Workshop on Modular and Open Multilingual NLP (MOOMIN 2024)

St. Julian's, Malta
21 March 2024

ISBN: 978-1-7138-9456-8

Printed from e-media with permission by:

Curran Associates, Inc.
57 Morehouse Lane
Red Hook, NY 12571

Some format issues inherent in the e-media version may also appear in this print version.

Association for Computational Linguistics
209 N. Eighth Street
Stroudsburg, Pennsylvania 18360

Phone: 1-570-476-8006
Fax: 1-570-476-0860

acl@aclweb.org

Additional copies of this publication are available from:

Curran Associates, Inc.
57 Morehouse Lane
Red Hook, NY 12571 USA
Phone: 845-758-0400
Fax: 845-758-2633
Email: curran@proceedings.com
Web: www.proceedings.com

Workshop on Modular and Open Multilingual NLP (MOOMIN 2024)

Proceedings of the Workshop

March 21, 2024

Association for Computational Linguistics (ACL)
209 N. Eighth Street
Stroudsburg, PA 18360
USA
Tel: +1-570-476-8006
Fax: +1-570-476-0860
acl@aclweb.org

Introduction

Welcome to the 1st Workshop Proceedings on Modular and Open Multilingual NLP (MOOMIN)". The workshop will take place at EACL 2024 in Malta on March 21st.

The MOOMIN workshop's aim is to bring together researchers and NLP practitioners interested in modular approaches to the design of natural language systems. This trend of research is a direct reply to the challenges and opportunities of monolithic large language models: To keep our field sustainable, we need models that are reusable, adaptable, and repurposable. We invited paper submissions on various topics, including Mixture-of-Expert models, modular pre-training of multilingual language and translation models, techniques that leverage adapters and hypernetworks, modular extensions of existing NLP models systems, and especially welcome work focusing on low-resource settings.

We have curated the MOOMIN workshop program to encourage discussions that will lead to valuable insights into the workshop topics. On the day of the workshop, there will be a total of 9 oral presentations of papers that offer innovative approaches and solutions to the challenges of scalability, language coverage, efficiency and re-usability of large language models. Of these 9 presentations, 5 correspond to archival papers published in the workshop proceedings, 1 is a non-archival submission and 3 papers are coming from this years' EACL Findings. The overall acceptance rate of archival submissions was 62.5%. In addition, we also invited two keynote speakers, Edoardo M. Ponti and Angela Fan, whose works have had remarkable impact in the field of modular NLP.

We are grateful to all authors, reviewers, and participants who contributed to the success of this workshop. We would also like to thank the European Research Council and the Research Council of Finland for their support of the workshop through the FoTran project (grant agreement no. 771113) and the GreenNLP project, respectively.

The MOOMIN organizers,

Timothee Mickus, Jörg Tiedemann, Ahmet Üstün, Raúl Vázquez & Ivan Vulić

Program Committee

Program Chairs

Timothee Mickus, University of Helsinki
Jörg Tiedemann, University of Helsinki
Ivan Vulić, University of Cambridge and PolyAI Limited
Raúl Vázquez, University of Helsinki
Ahmet Üstün, Cohere For Ai

Publication Chair

Raúl Vázquez, University of Helsinki

Invited Speakers

Edoardo M. Ponti, University of Edinburgh and University of Cambridge
Angela Fan, Meta AI Research, FAIR

Reviewers

David Ifeoluwa Adelani, University College London
Alan Ansell, University of Cambridge
Lucas Caccia, McGill University
Hande Celikkanat, University of Helsinki
Alexandra Chronopoulou, Ludwig-Maximilians-Universität München
Mathias Creutz, University of Helsinki
Marzieh Fadaee, Cohere For AI
Stig-Arne Grönroos, University of Helsinki
Barry Haddow, University of Edinburgh
Shaoxiong Ji, University of Helsinki
Julia Kreutzer, Cohere for AI
Andrey Kutuzov, University of Oslo
Niki Andreas Loppi, NVIDIA
Kelly Marchisio, Cohere and Cohere
Benjamin Minixhofer, University of Cambridge
Joakim Nivre, Uppsala University
Clifton A Poth, Cohere and Technische Universität Darmstadt
Taido Purason, University of Tartu
Alessandro Raganato, University of Milan - Bicocca
Fabian David Schmidt, Bayerische Julius-Maximilians-Universität Würzburg
Miikka Silfverberg, University of British Columbia
Teemu Vahtola, University of Helsinki

Keynote Talk: Efficiency as an Inductive Bias for Language Learning

Edoardo M. Ponti
University of Edinburgh and University of Cambridge
2024-03-21 09:30:00 – Room: **Room 1**

Abstract: Efficiency in Natural Language Processing is often hailed as a solution to democratise access to AI technology and to make it more environmentally sustainable. In this talk, I emphasise an additional and sometimes neglected advantage of efficiency: namely, providing an inductive bias for language use and acquisition closer to those in humans, where efficiency trade-offs shape the very structure of language. I will start by recapitulating the main aspects of efficiency in deep learning, which are partly interconnected: time, memory, and parameter efficiency. Next, I will explore how efficient designs in state-of-the-art Large Language Models (a) may also act as inductive biases that improve their performance (b). For instance: (1a) Jointly learning to model and segment text allows for merging contiguous groups of token representations in intermediate layers, which reduces time and memory requirements. (1b) In addition, it also leads to learning (possibly reusable and hierarchical) abstractions from raw data, which further increase the model's predictive abilities; (2a) Learning parameter-efficient modules allows for fine-tuning LLMs with limited memory budgets. (2b) In addition, composing these specialised modules through appropriate routing also leads to better generalisation. In particular, I will show how modules can be implemented as highly composable sparse adapters and how routing through modules can be learned automatically. In conclusion, efficient designs of LLMs yield unexpected benefits, such as the ability to learn abstractions, adapt fast, and integrate disparate sources of knowledge.

Bio: Edoardo M. Ponti is a Lecturer (Assistant Professor) in Natural Language Processing at the University of Edinburgh, where he is part of the Institute for Language, Cognition, and Computation (ILCC), and an Affiliated Lecturer at the University of Cambridge. Previously, he was a visiting postdoctoral scholar at Stanford University and a postdoctoral fellow at Mila and McGill University in Montreal. In 2021, he obtained a PhD in computational linguistics from the University of Cambridge, St John's College. His main research foci are modular deep learning, sample-efficient learning, faithful text generation, computational typology and multilingual NLP. His research earned him a Google Research Faculty Award and 2 Best Paper Awards at EMNLP 2021 and RepL4NLP 2019. He is a board member and co-founder of SIGTYP, the ACL special interest group for computational typology, and a scholar of the European Lab for Learning and Intelligent Systems (ELLIS). He is a (terrible) violinist, football player, and an aspiring practitioner of heroic viticulture.

Keynote Talk: No Language Left Behind - Scaling Human-Centered Machine Translation

Angela Fan
Meta AI Research, FAIR
2024-03-21 16:00:00 – Room: **Room 2**

Abstract: Driven by the goal of eradicating language barriers on a global scale, machine translation has solidified itself as a key focus of artificial intelligence research today. However, such efforts have coalesced around a small subset of languages, leaving behind the vast majority of mostly low-resource languages. What does it take to break the 200 language barrier while ensuring safe, high-quality results, all while keeping ethical considerations in mind? In this talk, I introduce No Language Left Behind, an initiative to break language barriers for low-resource languages. In No Language Left Behind, we took on the low-resource language translation challenge by first contextualizing the need for translation support through exploratory interviews with native speakers. Then, we created datasets and models aimed at narrowing the performance gap between low and high-resource languages. We proposed multiple architectural and training improvements to counteract overfitting while training on thousands of tasks. Critically, we evaluated the performance of over 40,000 different translation directions using a human-translated benchmark, Flores-200, and combined human evaluation with a novel toxicity benchmark covering all languages in Flores-200 to assess translation safety. Our model achieves an improvement of 44% BLEU relative to the previous state-of-the-art, laying important groundwork towards realizing a universal translation system in an open-source manner.

Bio: Angela is a research scientist at Meta AI Research in New York, focusing on research in text generation. Currently, Angela works on language modeling and developing the line AI Agents Meta products. Recent research projects include No Language Left Behind, Universal Speech Translation for Unwritten Languages, and Llama2.

Table of Contents

Program

Thursday, March 21, 2024

09:15 - 09:30 *Opening Remarks*

09:30 - 10:30 *Keynote 1: Edoardo M. Ponti*

10:30 - 11:00 *Coffee Break*

11:00 - 12:20 *Session 1: Efficient use of Adapters*

The Impact of Language Adapters in Cross-Lingual Transfer for NLU
Jenny Kunz and Oskar Holmström

Modular Adaptation of Multilingual Encoders to Written Swiss German Dialect
Jannis Vamvas, Noëmi Aepli and Rico Sennrich

Less is Fed More: Sparsity Reduces Feature Distortion in Federated Learning
Aashiq Muhamed, Harshita Diddee and Abhinav Rao

Toward the Modular Training of Controlled Paraphrase Adapters
Teemu Vahtola and Mathias Creutz

12:20 - 14:00 *Lunch Break*

14:00 - 15:00 *Session 2: Selection and weighting of modules*

Mixing and Matching: Combining Independently Trained Translation Model Components
Taido Purason, Andre Tättar and Mark Fishel

Sequence Shortening for Context-Aware Machine Translation
Paweł Maka, Yusuf Can Semerci, Jan Scholtes and Gerasimos Spanakis

What the Weight?! A Unified Framework for Zero-Shot Knowledge Composition
Carolin Holtermann, Markus Frohmann, Navid Rekabsaz and Anne Lauscher

Thursday, March 21, 2024 (continued)

15:00 - 15:40	*Session 3: Tuning LLMs*
	Soft Prompt Tuning for Cross-Lingual Transfer: When Less is More Fred Philippy, Siwen Guo, Shohreh Haddadan, Cedric Lothritz, Jacques Klein and Tegawendé F. Bissyandé
	Monolingual or Multilingual Instruction Tuning: Which Makes a Better Alpaca Pinzhen Chen, Shaoxiong Ji, Nikolay Bogoychev, Andrey Kutuzov, Barry Haddow and Kenneth Heafield
15:40 - 16:00	*Coffee Break*
16:00 - 17:00	*Keynote 2: Angela Fan*
17:00 - 17:20	*Closing Remarks*

Toward the Modular Training of Controlled Paraphrase Adapters

Teemu Vahtola and **Mathias Creutz**
Department of Digital Humanities
Faculty of Arts
University of Helsinki
Finland
{teemu.vahtola, mathias.creutz}@helsinki.fi

Abstract

Controlled paraphrase generation often focuses on a specific aspect of paraphrasing, for instance syntactically controlled paraphrase generation. However, these models face a limitation: they lack modularity. Consequently adapting them for another aspect, such as lexical variation, needs full retraining of the model each time. To enhance the flexibility in training controlled paraphrase models, our proposition involves incrementally training a modularized system for controlled paraphrase generation for English. We start by fine-tuning a pretrained language model to learn the broad task of paraphrase generation, generally emphasizing meaning preservation and surface form variation. Subsequently, we train a specialized sub-task adapter with limited sub-task specific training data. We can then leverage this adapter in guiding the paraphrase generation process toward a desired output aligning with the distinctive features within the sub-task training data.

The preliminary results on comparing the fine-tuned and adapted model against various competing systems indicates that the most successful method for mastering both general paraphrasing skills and task-specific expertise follows a two-stage approach. This approach involves starting with the initial fine-tuning of a generic paraphrase model and subsequently tailoring it for the specific sub-task.

1 Introduction

Paraphrase generation aims to produce sentences that maintain high semantic similarity with the source sentence, while deviating enough from it on surface form. Commonly used sequence-to-sequence models encounter challenges in generating diverse paraphrase outputs (Kumar et al., 2019). As a result, recent research in paraphrase generation has shifted toward controlled generation methods. These approaches condition the model on predefined qualities to produce specific outputs, aiming to overcome this limitation. Exploring approaches to controlled text generation has both theoretical and practical implications. It can influence the theoretical understanding of automatic language generation and offer practical applications across various domains and industries.

Through leveraging controlled text generation, models can for instance be steered to produce language that better follows user preferences (Fan et al., 2018). With enough surface form variation, paraphrasing can be useful in question answering (Dong et al., 2017), data augmentation (Kumar et al., 2019), and machine translation (Callison-Burch et al., 2006; Mehdizadeh Seraj et al., 2015), among other tasks. Even if trained to perform certain paraphrase transformations, recent controlled paraphrase generation systems are limited in flexibility. Incorporating an additional control feature necessitates retraining the entire model. To overcome this limitation, we make the assumption that paraphrase generation essentially behaves in a modular manner. To evaluate our assumption, we propose the training of a modular system for controlled paraphrase generation through initial fine-tuning or broader task adapters (Pfeiffer et al., 2020b) followed by more specialized sub-task adapters. Hence, in contrast to standard fine-tuning of all parameters of a model, we initially train the model to perform the necessary paraphrasing skills, namely meaning preservation and surface form variation, and further refine the model in a modular way to produce outputs that encompass some desired paraphrase nuances. We focus on English paraphrasing, incorporating one specific aspect of paraphrasing, namely antonym substitution (Bhagat and Hovy, 2013). We select this paraphrase operation due to the availability of a specialized test suite designed for evaluating paraphrase models on sentence pairs that incorporate antonym substitution (Vahtola et al., 2022), enabling systematic comparison of various experimental setups. However,

Proceedings of the 1st Workshop on Modular and Open Multilingual NLP (MOOMIN 2024), pages 1–6
March 21, 2024

our proposed approach could as well be applied to other paraphrase phenomena and languages where paraphrase data is available.

2 Previous Research

Common methods for automatic paraphrase generation rely on sequence-to-sequence modeling, often leveraging machine translation (Tiedemann and Scherrer, 2019; Thompson and Post, 2020; Sun et al., 2022, *inter alia*), or monolingual parallel data (Prakash et al., 2016; Sjöblom et al., 2020). These models, however, often struggle with generating sufficient variation (Kumar et al., 2020). As a result, increased emphasis has been given to generating controlled paraphrases, specifically targeting variations across predefined dimensions.

There has been significant research attention directed toward controlled paraphrasing in various granularity levels, from aiming to produce lexical variation by providing synonym substitutions (Fu et al., 2019) to the generation of syntactically controlled paraphrases (Iyyer et al., 2018; Kumar et al., 2020; Sun et al., 2021). While these approaches are constrained by concentrating solely on one level of detail, diverse paraphrasing encompasses multiple levels of granularity. To acknowledge this limitation, Huang et al. (2019) use dictionaries to perform word-level and phrase-level paraphrasing, obtaining more variation. Vahtola et al. (2023) train a multilingual NMT model with control tokens related to various aspects of paraphrasing. It is still however an open question how the control tokens interplay. In addition, a critical limitation arises with these models: they lack modularity, wherein all control tokens exert simultaneous influence on the output, making it impossible to selectively deactivate any subset of control features during the inference process or flexibly adapt the model to new features. In contrast, we propose the training of a modular controlled paraphrase generation model leveraging adapter transformations (Houlsby et al., 2019; Pfeiffer et al., 2020b).

In addition to being widely studied for cross-lingual transfer (e.g., Pfeiffer et al., 2020b) and NMT (Üstün et al., 2021), modular and parameter efficient fine-tuning has been explored in other sequence-to-sequence tasks. Bapna and Firat (2019) use a modification of trainable adapter blocks (Houlsby et al., 2019) to adapt MT outputs for new languages and domains. Wan et al. (2023) leverage prefix-tuning for generating syntactically controlled paraphrases. In contrast to the previous work on modular fine-tuning, our focus lies in the modular training paradigm specific to paraphrasing. We delve into training specialized sub-task adapters within this single task. These adapters are supposed to capture task and sub-task specific information, and are to be assembled to produce controlled paraphrasing toward an intended output.

3 Data

We use the English partition of the Opusparcus paraphrase dataset (Creutz, 2018) for alternately fine-tuning the full model or training a generic paraphrase adapter. The training data in Opusparcus was automatically constructed and organized to prioritize the most probable paraphrastic sentence pairs at the beginning, with decreasing likelihood of being paraphrases as the data progresses. Hence, we select the first 1 000 000 sentence pairs from the corpus as training data, denoted as T, comprising approximately of 95% of true paraphrases (Creutz, 2018), and use the sentence pairs annotated as paraphrases from the Opusparcus development set for tuning the models. Moreover, within the training set T, we extract a specialized subset $T_n \subset T$ consisting of 12 870 examples. We use the first 12 000 examples as training data and save the final 870 examples to serve as a development set for tuning the specialized systems. This subset exclusively comprises instances where an explicit negation token is present in the target but absent in the source, and is used for training a dedicated sub-task adapter as a part of a broader paraphrasing task. We aim to extract sentences that demonstrate interesting paraphrastic relationships through the use of negation or negated antonymy, as opposed to sentences that negate the intended meaning. We release the task-specific data in `https://github.com/teemuvh/controlled-paraphrase-adapters`.

4 Experiments

Our objective is to incrementally train and assemble a modular system for controlled paraphrase generation. We undertake training and assessment across several models. To start, we establish a baseline by fine-tuning `flan-t5-base`[1] (Chung et al., 2022) using a set of 1 000 000 paraphrase pairs (T) sourced from the English partition of the Opusparcus training set. Furthermore, we fine-tune a sepa-

[1]The prefix we use for training and evaluating the models is: *paraphrase this sentence:*.

Original	Candidates
You're not fat.	You're not thin., You're fat., **You're thin.**
It's not fair.	It's not unfair., It's fair., **It's unfair.**
This is not a good idea.	This is not a bad idea., This is a good idea., **This is a bad idea.**
It is not safe.	It is not dangerous., It is safe., **It is dangerous.**

Table 1: Examples from the SemAntoNeg test suite. The true paraphrase to the input sentence is highlighted.

rate system using only a subset of the training data (T_n) that comprises of examples incorporating paraphrasing through negation and negated antonymy, extracted from the complete training set. We also perform a two-stage fine-tuning, starting with fine-tuning the base model with T, and sequentially fine-tuning with T_n.

In all adapter experiments, we leverage the adapter-transformers library (Pfeiffer et al., 2020a). We optimize modular fine-tuning by utilizing the bottleneck adapter (Houlsby et al., 2019) configuration proposed in Pfeiffer et al. (2020b) in conjunction with the base model. We then proceed to train two task adapters: one using the entire training dataset (T) for a broad paraphrasing task, and another using a subset (T_n) of the data for a specific controlled paraphrasing sub-task. Finally, we explore incremental adapter training by enhancing the base model with the paraphrase adapter. We then freeze the weights of the base model and the paraphrase adapter and proceed to train an additional sub-task adapter. This adapter not only benefits from the paraphrase adapter's information but also focuses on learning more specific paraphrasing transformations incorporating negation and antonym substitution. We train each system on a single GPU for 3 epochs with a batch size of 128, and 5e-5 learning rate.

We evaluate the models on a dedicated test suite designed for paraphrase detection within sequences incorporating negated antonyms (Vahtola et al., 2022). The test suite is intended to be used to evaluate models on a difficult paraphrase detection task involving sequences with high lexical overlap. Examples of the data are provided in Table 1. To make the test suite suitable for evaluating sequence-to-sequence models, we extract each source sentence and its true paraphrase, i.e., the third candidate as highlighted in the examples in Table 1, from the test suite. By treating these extracted pairs as source-target sequences, we reframe the task as a sequence-to-sequence challenge. A successful model hence performs antonym substitution to produce a paraphrase of the original sentence. Controlled paraphrasing aims to replicate a specific output sentence while incorporating predefined control features. Therefore, we decide to evaluate the models using BLEU (Papineni et al., 2002) with respect to the references and to the inputs. We use sacreBLEU (Post, 2018) for calculating the BLEU scores.

5 Results

Table 2 presents the results. The base model evaluation (denoted as base in Table 2), conducted without any fine-tuning or adaptation, establishes a baseline BLEU score of 25.07. Fine-tuning (para-ft) or training an adapter (para-adapt) solely with the 1 000 000 examples (T from now on) yields suboptimal results (14–17 BLEU) on the negated antonym test data. However, this outcome is expected, as the model is not explicitly trained to handle paraphrases with negation or negated antonyms. While the BLEU score may be lower for the paraphrase models, it doesn't necessarily imply inferiority in their ability to paraphrase. As indicated by the high BLEU score with respect to the source sentence (S-BLEU in Table 2), the base model without fine-tuning or adapter training has a high tendency to copy the input sentence, consequently yielding relatively high BLEU score in this task owing to the extensive lexical overlap found within the test data examples. The dedicated paraphrase models aim to introduce more alternations to the inputs, resulting in lower BLEU scores despite potentially producing true paraphrases.

Fully fine-tuning the model with the filtered subset (T_n) of the training data (neg-ft), thus highlighting paraphrasing through negation and antonymy, consistently produces higher BLEU scores on the task compared to both the base model and models trained solely on T. Adapter training on top of the base model using T_n (neg-adapt) results in even higher BLEU scores. Parameter efficient fine-tuning has been shown to be effective in low-resource scenarios (e.g., Karimi Mahabadi

Model	BLEU	S-BLEU
base	25.07	95.23
para-ft	14.21	30.73
para-adapt	17.15	47.71
neg-ft	30.24	49.15
neg-adapt	32.79	57.92
para-ft+neg-ft	23.40	24.83
para-adapt+neg-adapt	26.06	36.45
para-ft+neg-adapt	34.00	66.45

Table 2: Results of the different models on the SemAntoNeg challenge set framed as a sequence-to-sequence task. Here, BLEU scores measure the alignment with reference sentences, whereas S-BLEU assesses alignment with the input itself.

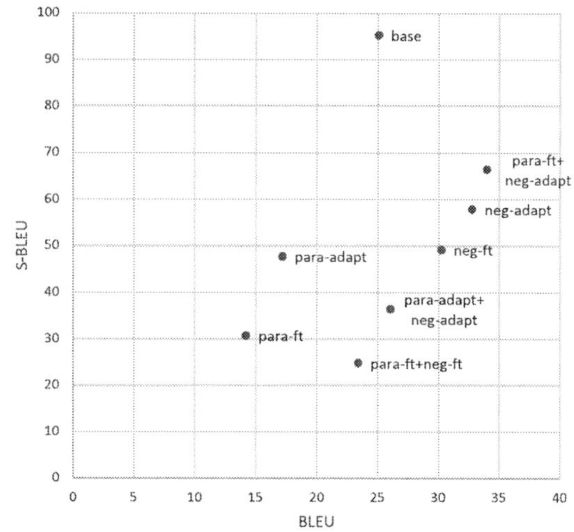

Figure 1: The BLEU and S-BLEU values of the methods shown graphically. The best performing models are assumed to show far to the right, reflecting a high BLEU with respect to the reference, and at around 25 % S-BLEU, which is the BLEU value of the reference with respect to the source. That is, an oracle model that would produce the desired reference sentences would obtain BLEU = 100 % and S-BLEU = 24.90 %.

et al., 2021), which might explain why the adapter method achieves higher BLEU scores compared to full fine-tuning when trained specifically for the given paraphrasing sub-task.

Initiating training by fine-tuning a generic paraphrase model, followed by further fine-tuning with the specific sub-task data yields a subpar model (para-ft+neg-ft). Similarly, training an extensive paraphrase adapter before introducing a specialized sub-task adapter (para-adapt+neg-adapt) results in a model which barely surpasses the base model's performance when evaluated against the reference using BLEU. Comparing the outputs to the input sentences however shows that the incrementally adapted model achieves similar BLEU scores as the base model by trying to produce variation rather than simply duplicating the input sentence, as indicated by the lower S-BLEU score of the adapted model.

The best BLEU scores are obtained by fully fine-tuning the base model leveraging all 1 000 000 paraphrase examples and training a specialized sub-task adapter on top of the refined model (para-ft+neg-adapt). We hypothesize that the initial fine-tuning steers the model toward generating outputs that highly resemble the input, reflected in a relatively high S-BLEU. Subsequent adapter training on a smaller scale then refines the model's proficiency in paraphrase operations involving negation and negated antonyms, as indicated by the highest BLEU.

The relationship between the obtained BLEU and S-BLEU is presented in Figure 1. A robust paraphrase model would typically demonstrate a balance between a higher BLEU score and a lower S-BLEU score, positioning itself toward the lower right corner of the diagram. This would indicate robustness by demonstrating a substantial lexical similarity between the input and the reference, while having a lesser alignment with the input itself. In our task, an oracle model producing the exact reference sentence would obtain 100 BLEU and 24.90 S-BLEU.

To summarize the results, the base model along with the models subjected to plain fine-tuning or adaptation with the more generic paraphrase data exhibit poor performance, highlighted by the base model's high S-BLEU, and the low BLEU scores achieved by the fine-tuned or adapted models. Incorporating specialized training for the intended paraphrasing task, either through fine-tuning or adaptation, is essential for success in the task. However, the results obtained with the models specifically trained for paraphrasing through negation or negated antonymy remain somewhat inconclusive. Further analysis is necessary to determine the optimal training configuration for assembling general paraphrasing capabilities with specialized sub-task capabilities. Additionally, we hypothesize that parameter-efficient fine-tuning is better suited in scenarios involving limited data. However, the limited training data is also more task-specific, so it is still too early to draw general conclusions.

6 Conclusions

We propose the training of a modular paraphrase generation model that is built incrementally. This model starts by fine-tuning on a robust pretrained language model to learn the general requirements of paraphrase generation, namely meaning preservation and surface form variation. Subsequently, we train a specialized sub-task adapter with a limited number of sub-task specific training data to guide the paraphrase generation process toward a desired output. We compare the model involving fine-tuning followed by sub-task adaptation to several counterparts, including a base model without further training, as well as differently fine-tuned or adapted systems.

When assessing on a dedicated test set involving paraphrasing with negation or negated antonyms, we find that the most effective approach for learning both general paraphrasing abilities and sub-task specific expertise is achieved by fully fine-tuning a model for paraphrasing and then tailoring it to the specific sub-task through modular updates.

In future work, we wish to delve deeper into modularity for controlled paraphrasing. We intend to expand the model's capabilities by incrementally training it to encompass additional paraphrasing nuances, such as syntactic or lexical variation. Furthermore, we would like to assess how varying the size and task-specificity of the training data impacts the results. Finally, we would like to extend our approach to a multilingual setup.

Acknowledgements

This study was supported by the Behind the Words project, funded by the Research Council of Finland. We wish to acknowledge CSC – The Finnish IT Center for Science for the computational resources they have generously provided. We express our gratitude to Ivan Vulić for engaging in insightful discussions and providing valuable feedback during the conceptualization of this work.

References

Ankur Bapna and Orhan Firat. 2019. Simple, scalable adaptation for neural machine translation. In *Proceedings of the 2019 Conference on Empirical Methods in Natural Language Processing and the 9th International Joint Conference on Natural Language Processing (EMNLP-IJCNLP)*, pages 1538–1548, Hong Kong, China. Association for Computational Linguistics.

Rahul Bhagat and Eduard Hovy. 2013. Squibs: What is a paraphrase? *Computational Linguistics*, 39(3):463–472.

Chris Callison-Burch, Philipp Koehn, and Miles Osborne. 2006. Improved statistical machine translation using paraphrases. In *Proceedings of the Human Language Technology Conference of the NAACL, Main Conference*, pages 17–24, New York City, USA. Association for Computational Linguistics.

Hyung Won Chung, Le Hou, Shayne Longpre, Barret Zoph, Yi Tay, William Fedus, Yunxuan Li, Xuezhi Wang, Mostafa Dehghani, Siddhartha Brahma, et al. 2022. Scaling instruction-finetuned language models. *arXiv preprint arXiv:2210.11416*.

Mathias Creutz. 2018. Open subtitles paraphrase corpus for six languages. In *Proceedings of the Eleventh International Conference on Language Resources and Evaluation (LREC 2018)*, Miyazaki, Japan. European Language Resources Association (ELRA).

Li Dong, Jonathan Mallinson, Siva Reddy, and Mirella Lapata. 2017. Learning to paraphrase for question answering. In *Proceedings of the 2017 Conference on Empirical Methods in Natural Language Processing*, pages 875–886, Copenhagen, Denmark. Association for Computational Linguistics.

Angela Fan, David Grangier, and Michael Auli. 2018. Controllable abstractive summarization. In *Proceedings of the 2nd Workshop on Neural Machine Translation and Generation*, pages 45–54, Melbourne, Australia. Association for Computational Linguistics.

Yao Fu, Yansong Feng, and John P Cunningham. 2019. Paraphrase generation with latent bag of words. *Advances in Neural Information Processing Systems*, 32.

Neil Houlsby, Andrei Giurgiu, Stanislaw Jastrzebski, Bruna Morrone, Quentin De Laroussilhe, Andrea Gesmundo, Mona Attariyan, and Sylvain Gelly. 2019. Parameter-efficient transfer learning for nlp. In *International Conference on Machine Learning*, pages 2790–2799. PMLR.

Shaohan Huang, Yu Wu, Furu Wei, and Zhongzhi Luan. 2019. Dictionary-guided editing networks for paraphrase generation. In *Proceedings of the AAAI Conference on Artificial Intelligence*, volume 33, pages 6546–6553.

Mohit Iyyer, John Wieting, Kevin Gimpel, and Luke Zettlemoyer. 2018. Adversarial example generation with syntactically controlled paraphrase networks. In *Proceedings of the 2018 Conference of the North American Chapter of the Association for Computational Linguistics: Human Language Technologies, Volume 1 (Long Papers)*, pages 1875–1885, New Orleans, Louisiana. Association for Computational Linguistics.

Rabeeh Karimi Mahabadi, James Henderson, and Sebastian Ruder. 2021. Compacter: Efficient low-rank hypercomplex adapter layers. *Advances in Neural Information Processing Systems*, 34:1022–1035.

Ashutosh Kumar, Kabir Ahuja, Raghuram Vadapalli, and Partha Talukdar. 2020. Syntax-guided controlled generation of paraphrases. *Transactions of the Association for Computational Linguistics*, 8:329–345.

Ashutosh Kumar, Satwik Bhattamishra, Manik Bhandari, and Partha Talukdar. 2019. Submodular optimization-based diverse paraphrasing and its effectiveness in data augmentation. In *Proceedings of the 2019 Conference of the North American Chapter of the Association for Computational Linguistics: Human Language Technologies, Volume 1 (Long and Short Papers)*, pages 3609–3619, Minneapolis, Minnesota. Association for Computational Linguistics.

Ramtin Mehdizadeh Seraj, Maryam Siahbani, and Anoop Sarkar. 2015. Improving statistical machine translation with a multilingual paraphrase database. In *Proceedings of the 2015 Conference on Empirical Methods in Natural Language Processing*, pages 1379–1390, Lisbon, Portugal. Association for Computational Linguistics.

Kishore Papineni, Salim Roukos, Todd Ward, and Wei-Jing Zhu. 2002. Bleu: a method for automatic evaluation of machine translation. In *Proceedings of the 40th Annual Meeting of the Association for Computational Linguistics*, pages 311–318, Philadelphia, Pennsylvania, USA. Association for Computational Linguistics.

Jonas Pfeiffer, Andreas Rücklé, Clifton Poth, Aishwarya Kamath, Ivan Vulić, Sebastian Ruder, Kyunghyun Cho, and Iryna Gurevych. 2020a. Adapterhub: A framework for adapting transformers. In *Proceedings of the 2020 Conference on Empirical Methods in Natural Language Processing: System Demonstrations*, pages 46–54.

Jonas Pfeiffer, Ivan Vulić, Iryna Gurevych, and Sebastian Ruder. 2020b. MAD-X: An Adapter-Based Framework for Multi-Task Cross-Lingual Transfer. In *Proceedings of the 2020 Conference on Empirical Methods in Natural Language Processing (EMNLP)*, pages 7654–7673, Online. Association for Computational Linguistics.

Matt Post. 2018. A call for clarity in reporting BLEU scores. In *Proceedings of the Third Conference on Machine Translation: Research Papers*, pages 186–191, Brussels, Belgium. Association for Computational Linguistics.

Aaditya Prakash, Sadid A. Hasan, Kathy Lee, Vivek Datla, Ashequl Qadir, Joey Liu, and Oladimeji Farri. 2016. Neural paraphrase generation with stacked residual LSTM networks. In *Proceedings of COLING 2016, the 26th International Conference on Computational Linguistics: Technical Papers*, pages 2923–2934, Osaka, Japan. The COLING 2016 Organizing Committee.

Eetu Sjöblom, Mathias Creutz, and Yves Scherrer. 2020. Paraphrase generation and evaluation on colloquial-style sentences. In *Proceedings of the Twelfth Language Resources and Evaluation Conference*, pages 1814–1822, Marseille, France. European Language Resources Association.

Jiao Sun, Xuezhe Ma, and Nanyun Peng. 2021. AESOP: Paraphrase generation with adaptive syntactic control. In *Proceedings of the 2021 Conference on Empirical Methods in Natural Language Processing*, pages 5176–5189, Online and Punta Cana, Dominican Republic. Association for Computational Linguistics.

Xiaofei Sun, Yufei Tian, Yuxian Meng, Nanyun Peng, Fei Wu, Jiwei Li, and Chun Fan. 2022. Paraphrase generation as unsupervised machine translation. In *Proceedings of the 29th International Conference on Computational Linguistics*, pages 6379–6391, Gyeongju, Republic of Korea. International Committee on Computational Linguistics.

Brian Thompson and Matt Post. 2020. Paraphrase generation as zero-shot multilingual translation: Disentangling semantic similarity from lexical and syntactic diversity. In *Proceedings of the Fifth Conference on Machine Translation*, pages 561–570, Online. Association for Computational Linguistics.

Jörg Tiedemann and Yves Scherrer. 2019. Measuring semantic abstraction of multilingual NMT with paraphrase recognition and generation tasks. In *Proceedings of the 3rd Workshop on Evaluating Vector Space Representations for NLP*, pages 35–42, Minneapolis, USA. Association for Computational Linguistics.

Ahmet Üstün, Alexandre Berard, Laurent Besacier, and Matthias Gallé. 2021. Multilingual unsupervised neural machine translation with denoising adapters. In *Proceedings of the 2021 Conference on Empirical Methods in Natural Language Processing*, pages 6650–6662, Online and Punta Cana, Dominican Republic. Association for Computational Linguistics.

Teemu Vahtola, Mathias Creutz, and Jörg Tiedemann. 2022. It is not easy to detect paraphrases: Analysing semantic similarity with antonyms and negation using the new SemAntoNeg benchmark. In *Proceedings of the Fifth BlackboxNLP Workshop on Analyzing and Interpreting Neural Networks for NLP*, pages 249–262, Abu Dhabi, United Arab Emirates (Hybrid). Association for Computational Linguistics.

Teemu Vahtola, Mathias Creutz, and Jrg Tiedemann. 2023. Guiding zero-shot paraphrase generation with fine-grained control tokens. In *Proceedings of the 12th Joint Conference on Lexical and Computational Semantics (*SEM 2023)*, pages 323–337, Toronto, Canada. Association for Computational Linguistics.

Yixin Wan, Kuan-Hao Huang, and Kai-Wei Chang. 2023. PIP: Parse-instructed prefix for syntactically controlled paraphrase generation. In *Findings of the Association for Computational Linguistics: ACL 2023*, pages 10372–10380, Toronto, Canada. Association for Computational Linguistics.

Soft Prompt Tuning for Cross-Lingual Transfer: When Less is More

Fred Philippy[1,2], Siwen Guo[1], Shohreh Haddadan[1],
Cedric Lothritz[2], Jacques Klein[2], Tegawendé F. Bissyandé[2]

[1] Zortify S.A., Luxembourg
[2] University of Luxembourg, Luxembourg
{fred, siwen}@zortify.com, shohreh.haddadan@gmail.com
{cedric.lothritz, jacques.klein, tegawende.bissyande}@uni.lu

Abstract

Soft Prompt Tuning (SPT) is a parameter-efficient method for adapting pre-trained language models (PLMs) to specific tasks by inserting learnable embeddings, or soft prompts, at the input layer of the PLM, without modifying its parameters. This paper investigates the potential of SPT for cross-lingual transfer. Unlike previous studies on SPT for cross-lingual transfer that often fine-tune both the soft prompt and the model parameters, we adhere to the original intent of SPT by keeping the model parameters frozen and only training the soft prompt. This does not only reduce the computational cost and storage overhead of full-model fine-tuning, but we also demonstrate that this very parameter efficiency intrinsic to SPT can enhance cross-lingual transfer performance to linguistically distant languages. Moreover, we explore how different factors related to the prompt, such as the length or its reparameterization, affect cross-lingual transfer performance.

1 Introduction

Fine-tuning pre-trained language models (PLMs) on task-specific labeled data requires large amounts of computational resources and may cause catastrophic forgetting of the pre-trained knowledge (Goodfellow et al., 2015). In multilingual settings, this may lead to poor cross-lingual transfer performance (Vu et al., 2022).

To address these challenges, Lester et al. (2021) introduced Soft Prompt Tuning (SPT), a method that inserts learnable embeddings, or soft prompts, at the PLM's input layer. The PLM then makes predictions using the output of its pre-trained language modeling head. The key advantage of SPT lies in its ability to leverage the pre-existing knowledge within PLMs while reducing the reliance on extensive task-specific fine-tuning. SPT has been shown to achieve remarkable results in various monolingual downstream tasks, especially in few-shot settings.

Motivated by this success, some recent works have also explored the use of SPT for cross-lingual transfer, where the goal is to leverage a multilingual language model (MLLM) to transfer knowledge from a high-resource to a low-resource language. However, these works have not fully exploited the potential of SPT. Some have appended a newly initialized classifier to the model (Tu et al., 2022; Park et al., 2023), hindering the suitability of SPT for few-shot learning. Others have fine-tuned the entire model along with the prompt (Zhao and Schütze, 2021; Huang et al., 2022), which reduces the computational efficiency of SPT.

This is especially problematic given the growing size of state-of-the-art language models. Therefore, we explore the impact on SPT's cross-lingual transfer performance when adhering to the original methodology of Lester et al. (2021), which involves fine-tuning only the soft prompt while keeping all model parameters frozen. Specifically, this paper contributes to the field of cross-lingual SPT by:

- Investigating the impact of model freezing on the cross-lingual transfer performance of few-shot SPT.
- Demonstrating that by freezing the model, SPT achieves enhanced cross-lingual transfer, especially to languages linguistically distant from the source language.
- Exploring further non-linguistic factors that influence the cross-lingual transfer performance of SPT, in particular prompt length and prompt reparameterization.

In this study, we conduct experiments on a topic classification dataset in 52 different languages and using 4 different models in few-shot settings. We believe that our findings can improve the existing methods that aim to enhance cross-lingual SPT, particularly in the context of current state-of-the-art models with billions of parameters where parameter efficiency is crucial.

Proceedings of the 1st Workshop on Modular and Open Multilingual NLP (MOOMIN 2024), pages 7–15
March 21, 2024

2 Related Work

Lester et al. (2021) proposed SPT, a method to leverage a PLM's pre-trained language modeling head without appending a new classifier. SPT relies on a soft prompt, which is a set of learnable embeddings that are concatenated with the input sequence, and keeps all other model parameters frozen. Since then, several recent works have explored the use of soft prompts for MLLMs. Zhao and Schütze (2021) first show that SPT outperforms fine-tuning in few-shot scenarios for cross-lingual transfer. Huang et al. (2022) introduce a method to train a language-agnostic soft prompt. However, unlike our study, none of these works on cross-lingual SPT employ model parameter freezing, leading to a reduced efficiency in their methods. In contrast, Tu et al. (2022) and Park et al. (2023) perform model freezing and, in corroboration with Zhao and Schütze (2021), also show that SPT outperforms fine-tuning for cross-lingual transfer. However, they append a newly initialized classification head to the model instead of using the PLM's pre-trained language modeling head, which diverges from the original idea of SPT. This setup is unsuitable for few-shot learning, requiring experiments to be conducted in full-data settings. In addition, prior studies often focus on smaller ranges of languages, which impedes making conclusive observations about SPT's cross-lingual tendencies across different languages and language families.

3 Experimental Setup

Besides adhering to the original setup of SPT, enabling parameter-efficient and data-efficient training, our study also sets itself apart in its objectives from the existing literature. Rather than simply demonstrating superior cross-lingual transfer performance of SPT over fine-tuning, our research aims to show that the minimal impact on the MLLM's representation space not only generally enhances transfer performance but is particularly effective for linguistically distant languages.

We provide more specific details on our experimental setup in Appendix A.

3.1 Soft Prompt

Following Lester et al. (2021), we append a soft prompt to the input sequence which is passed through an autoregressive language model, generating the logits for the next token in the input sequence. Each class is linked to a token from the model's vocabulary, enabling us to map the token with the highest logit to the predicted class. Such a mapping is referred to as the *verbalizer* (Figure 1).

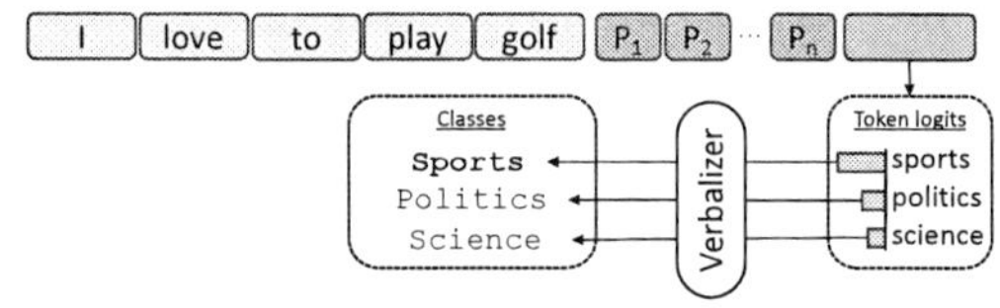

Figure 1: A simplified illustration of SPT (Lester et al., 2021). $P_1, \ldots, P_n$ denote the soft prompt tokens, with each token corresponding to a trainable embedding. Essentially, for a model with an embedding dimension d, a soft prompt of length n forms a $d \times n$ matrix.

3.2 Implementation Details

Models With the recent advancement and popularity of autoregressive language models for various tasks, our research is conducted using two types of MLLMs based on this architecture: XGLM (Lin et al., 2022) and BLOOM (Scao et al., 2022). For both models we use 2 different sizes: XGLM-564M and XGLM-1.7B for XGLM, and BLOOM-560M and BLOOM-1.1B for BLOOM.

Data In our study, we use SIB-200 (Adelani et al., 2023), a topic classification dataset containing seven distinct topics and covering a diverse range of 200 languages and dialects. We chose this dataset for its broader, more diverse language range compared to prior studies on cross-lingual SPT, covering almost all languages our models support, enabling more comprehensive observations.

Technical Details We compare two different settings: tuning the soft prompt with model freezing (*w/ MF*) and without model freezing (*w/o MF*). We perform few-shot fine-tuning only using English samples. The final cross-lingual transfer performance is then evaluated on the test sets of all languages supported by the respective model (30 for XGLM, 38 for BLOOM), using accuracy as the metric. We repeat each experiment 4 times with different random seeds and report the mean.

4 Results

We provide the full results across all models and languages in Appendix D. The results reveal that model freezing not only **boosts cross-lingual transfer performance** (Figure 2) but additionally is a step towards **closing the transfer gap** between linguistically distant and similar languages. This

		DATA	SYN	GEO	INV	GEN	PHON	FEA
BLOOM-560M	*w/o MF*	0,6781	0,6457	0,2294	0,3779	0,5081	**0,4343**	0,4221
	w/ MF	**0,6080**	**0,5742**	**0,2034**	**0,2629**	**0,3676**	0,4482	**0,3165**
BLOOM-1.1B	*w/o MF*	0,6788	0,6403	0,1693	0,4605	0,5679	0,5272	-0,4685
	w/ MF	**0,4856**	**0,4177**	**0,0290**	**0,2930**	**0,3711**	**0,4283**	**0,3002**
XGLM-564M	*w/o MF*	0,2672	0,6767	0,4694	0,4016	0,3203	0,4756	0,5949
	w/ MF	**0,2453**	**0,6574**	**0,2551**	**0,3410**	**0,2201**	**0,3285**	**0,5185**
XGLM-1.7B	*w/o MF*	0,2636	0,6722	**0,2566**	0,3623	0,2924	0,3213	0,5315
	w/ MF	**0,2560**	**0,6694**	0,2949	**0,3155**	**0,2786**	**0,2779**	**0,4922**

Table 1: Pearson correlation between (8-shot) cross-lingual transfer performance and 6 different linguistic similarity metrics, namely syntactic (SYN), geographic (GEO), inventory (INV), genetic (GEN), phonological (PHON) and featural (FEA) distance, as well as the language-specific pre-training corpus size (DATA).

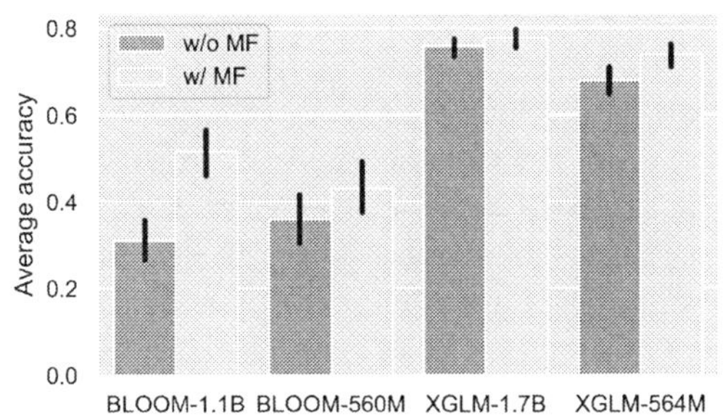

Figure 2: Average cross-lingual transfer performance of SPT with and without model freezing (MF) for different models across all languages supported by the respective model.

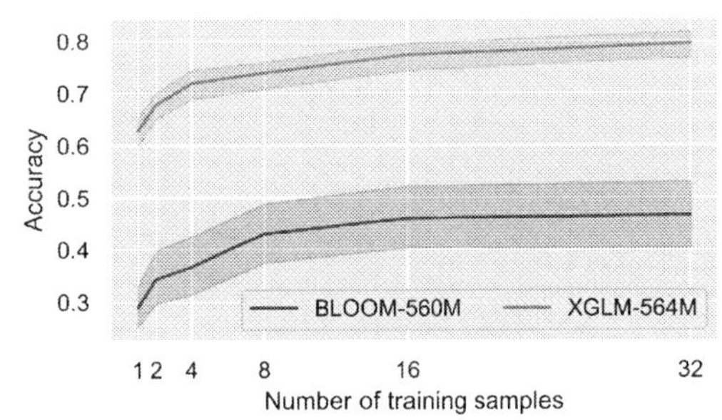

Figure 3: Average cross-lingual transfer performance of SPT with model freezing for different number of training samples per class.

can be seen in Table 1, which shows that the correlation strength between transfer performance and language similarity between source and target languages, measured using 6 different similarity metrics[1] (Littell et al., 2017), decreases when freezing model parameters. This suggests that the parameter efficiency of SPT mitigates the bias of cross-lingual transfer towards linguistically similar languages. In other words, by fine-tuning fewer parameters, cross-lingual transfer, especially to linguistically distant languages, is enhanced. This improvement over full-model fine-tuning may be attributed to the reduced impact on the MLLM's representation space during fine-tuning (Philippy et al., 2023).

Figure 3 also shows that, despite the limited number of tunable parameters when freezing all model parameters, additional training samples further boost cross-lingual transfer performance.

Parameter efficiency Besides better cross-lingual transfer performance, model freezing during SPT also provides parameter efficiency as fine-tuning is restricted to a number of soft prompt tokens, resulting in only a few thousand parameters in total. This is less than 0.01% of the parameters fine-tuned in previous studies (Zhao and Schütze, 2021; Huang et al., 2022).

For illustration, the storage requirement for a copy of the XGLM-1.7B model is approximately 3.2 GB, whereas a prompt needs less than 100KB. With respect to training duration, our observations indicate that the time required for training only the soft prompt is less than half compared to when training all model parameters. This benefit becomes even more pronounced when considering the increasing sizes of state-of-the-art models.

5 Impact of Prompt Length and Reparameterization

5.1 Prompt Length

Using the same configuration as described in Section 3.2, we compare the transfer performance of prompts with different lengths under the 8-shot setting. We consider prompt lengths in

[1]See Appendix B for more details.

$\{1, 2, 5, 10, 20, 30\}$ and report the results for all 4 models. Figure 4 shows that **if a soft prompt is too long, cross-lingual transfer performance degrades**.

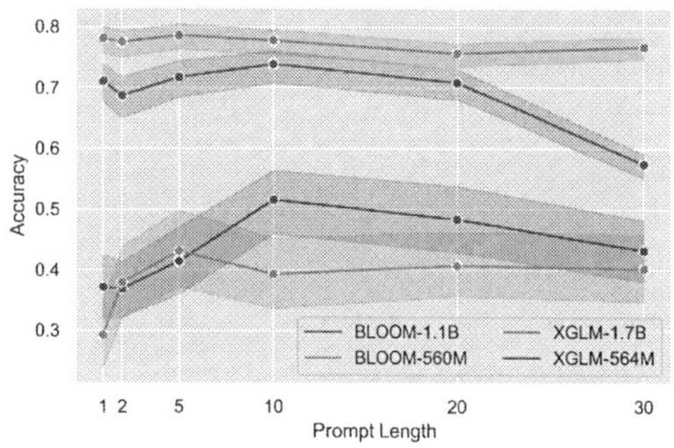

Figure 4: Average cross-lingual transfer performance, measured as accuracy, across different prompt lengths for different models.

5.2 Reparameterization

Direct fine-tuning of soft prompt embeddings may lead to unstable training and potentially reduces performance. To address this issue, previous works have proposed reparameterizing prompt embeddings using different architectures, such as an LSTM (Liu et al., 2021) or MLP (Li and Liang, 2021), which are fine-tuned along with the prompt embeddings. Liu et al. (2022) argue that reparameterization can also have negative effects depending on the task or dataset.

Motivated by this observation, we investigate the effect of reparameterization on cross-lingual transfer performance. We adopt the approach proposed by Razdaibiedina et al. (2023), which uses an MLP with a residual connection and a "bottleneck" layer for reparameterization. We provide further details on this method in Appendix C.

Our analysis reveals that BLOOM is significantly more affected by reparameterization than XGLM (Figure 5 in Appendix C). For both models, the **impact of reparameterization differs across languages** — being detrimental for some and advantageous for others. Notably, for BLOOM, Atlantic-Congo languages such as Yoruba, Twi, Kinyarwanda, Akan, Fon and Swahili experience the most significant performance decline due to reparameterization, with drops between 24% to 31%. Conversely, Indo-Aryan languages like Urdu, Hindi, Bengali, and Nepali, along with Dravidian languages like Malayalam and Tamil see the most significant improvements, with gains of up to 29%. For XGLM, the outcomes are more balanced. Nonetheless, we observe that the languages that benefit most from reparameterization either use Latin script, such as Haitian, German, and Turkish, or are Dravidian languages such as Telugu and Tamil.

Hence, we recommend that in cross-lingual settings, the decision to use or abstain from reparameterization should not be made uniformly. Instead, it should be tailored based on the specific target languages or language families in consideration.

6 Discussion

Previous works on SPT for cross-lingual transfer in few-shot settings suffers from two major drawbacks: 1) fine-tuning all model parameters along with the prompt reduces the computational efficiency of SPT; 2) a bias towards target languages that are linguistically closer to the source language. Our study tackles these issues by showing that by simply keeping model parameters frozen during SPT, we can make progress in addressing both these challenges.

Through our experiments, which covered a wider and more diverse range of languages than prior work on cross-lingual SPT, we observed intriguing effects of non-linguistic variables (such as model freezing, prompt length, and reparameterization) on the transfer performance for individual languages. Additionally, our results reveal language-specific differences that invite further inquiry into the possibility of tailoring prompts to the target language (e.g., applying prompt reparameterization or not depending on the linguistic distance between the target language family and the source language) rather than using a single prompt for universal transfer across languages. We believe that our findings will benefit future work on cross-lingual SPT and potentially improve the existing techniques (Huang et al., 2022), becoming more valuable as we adopt larger state-of-the-art models with billion- and trillion-scale parameters (Lester et al., 2021).

7 Conclusion

The objective of our study was to examine the impact of model freezing on the cross-lingual transfer performance of SPT. Our results demonstrate that SPT, a method that adjusts less than 0.01% of parameters compared to full-model fine-tuning, achieves comparable or superior performance for most target languages, particularly for those that are linguistically more distant. Furthermore, we found that shorter prompts enhance SPT's cross-lingual transfer performance, and that some target language families benefit from reparameterization while others are adversely affected by it.

Limitations

Our approach enhances transfer performance for several languages, especially those that are linguistically more distant. However, we also notice that it lowers the performance for some languages that are linguistically more similar. This limitation motivates us to pursue future research that aims to achieve balanced performance across languages

Another limitation of our approach is the instability of few-shot fine-tuning, which compromises the robustness of our method's evaluation. To mitigate this issue, we ran all experiments four times with different random seeds and reported the mean and variance of the results. However, we acknowledge that more research is needed to address the challenges of few-shot fine-tuning.

Ethics Statement

In this paper, we aim to improve the performance of MLLMs on low-resource languages, which often suffer from a lack of data and attention in NLP research. We believe that this is an important and ethical goal, as it enables NLP advances to benefit a broader range of language communities.

In addition, this paper aims to promote parameter efficiency, which is a crucial factor for reducing the computational and environmental costs of training and fine-tuning state-of-the-art language models. We believe that this aspect will enhance the accessibility and affordability of these models for researchers and practitioners who face computational constraints.

References

David Ifeoluwa Adelani, Hannah Liu, Xiaoyu Shen, Nikita Vassilyev, Jesujoba O. Alabi, Yanke Mao, Haonan Gao, and Annie En-Shiun Lee. 2023. SIB-200: A Simple, Inclusive, and Big Evaluation Dataset for Topic Classification in 200+ Languages and Dialects. ArXiv:2309.07445 [cs].

Chris Collins and Richard Kayne. 2011. *Syntactic Structures of the World's Languages*. New York University, New York.

Matthew S. Dryer and Martin Haspelmath. 2013. *WALS Online*. Max Planck Institute for Evolutionary Anthropology, Leipzig.

Ian J. Goodfellow, Mehdi Mirza, Da Xiao, Aaron Courville, and Yoshua Bengio. 2015. An Empirical Investigation of Catastrophic Forgetting in Gradient-Based Neural Networks. ArXiv:1312.6211 [cs, stat].

Harald Hammarström, Robert Forkel, Martin Haspelmath, and Sebastian Bank. 2015. *Glottolog 2.6*. Max Planck Institute for the Science of Human History, Jena.

Lianzhe Huang, Shuming Ma, Dongdong Zhang, Furu Wei, and Houfeng Wang. 2022. Zero-shot Cross-lingual Transfer of Prompt-based Tuning with a Unified Multilingual Prompt. In *Proceedings of the 2022 Conference on Empirical Methods in Natural Language Processing*, pages 11488–11497, Abu Dhabi, United Arab Emirates. Association for Computational Linguistics.

Brian Lester, Rami Al-Rfou, and Noah Constant. 2021. The Power of Scale for Parameter-Efficient Prompt Tuning. In *Proceedings of the 2021 Conference on Empirical Methods in Natural Language Processing*, pages 3045–3059, Online and Punta Cana, Dominican Republic. Association for Computational Linguistics.

M. Paul Lewis, Gary F. Simons, and Charles D. Fennig. 2015. *Ethnologue: Languages of the World, Eighteenth edition*. SIL International, Dallas, Texas.

Xiang Lisa Li and Percy Liang. 2021. Prefix-Tuning: Optimizing Continuous Prompts for Generation. In *Proceedings of the 59th Annual Meeting of the Association for Computational Linguistics and the 11th International Joint Conference on Natural Language Processing (Volume 1: Long Papers)*, pages 4582–4597, Online. Association for Computational Linguistics.

Xi Victoria Lin, Todor Mihaylov, Mikel Artetxe, Tianlu Wang, Shuohui Chen, Daniel Simig, Myle Ott, Naman Goyal, Shruti Bhosale, Jingfei Du, Ramakanth Pasunuru, Sam Shleifer, Punit Singh Koura, Vishrav Chaudhary, Brian O'Horo, Jeff Wang, Luke Zettlemoyer, Zornitsa Kozareva, Mona Diab, Veselin Stoyanov, and Xian Li. 2022. Few-shot Learning with Multilingual Generative Language Models. In *Proceedings of the 2022 Conference on Empirical Methods in Natural Language Processing*, pages 9019–9052, Abu Dhabi, United Arab Emirates. Association for Computational Linguistics.

Patrick Littell, David R. Mortensen, Ke Lin, Katherine Kairis, Carlisle Turner, and Lori Levin. 2017. URIEL and lang2vec: Representing languages as typological, geographical, and phylogenetic vectors. In *Proceedings of the 15th Conference of the European Chapter of the Association for Computational Linguistics: Volume 2, Short Papers*, pages 8–14, Valencia, Spain. Association for Computational Linguistics.

Xiao Liu, Kaixuan Ji, Yicheng Fu, Weng Tam, Zhengxiao Du, Zhilin Yang, and Jie Tang. 2022. P-Tuning: Prompt Tuning Can Be Comparable to Fine-tuning Across Scales and Tasks. In *Proceedings of the 60th Annual Meeting of the Association for Computational Linguistics (Volume 2: Short Papers)*, pages 61–68, Dublin, Ireland. Association for Computational Linguistics.

Xiao Liu, Yanan Zheng, Zhengxiao Du, Ming Ding, Yujie Qian, Zhilin Yang, and Jie Tang. 2021. GPT Understands, Too. ArXiv:2103.10385 [cs].

Steven Moran, Daniel McCloy, and (eds.). 2019. *PHOIBLE 2.0*. Max Planck Institute for the Science of Human History, Jena.

NLLB Team, Marta R. Costa-jussà, James Cross, Onur Çelebi, Maha Elbayad, Kenneth Heafield, Kevin Heffernan, Elahe Kalbassi, Janice Lam, Daniel Licht, Jean Maillard, Anna Sun, Skyler Wang, Guillaume Wenzek, Al Youngblood, Bapi Akula, Loic Barrault, Gabriel Mejia Gonzalez, Prangthip Hansanti, John Hoffman, Semarley Jarrett, Kaushik Ram Sadagopan, Dirk Rowe, Shannon Spruit, Chau Tran, Pierre Andrews, Necip Fazil Ayan, Shruti Bhosale, Sergey Edunov, Angela Fan, Cynthia Gao, Vedanuj Goswami, Francisco Guzmán, Philipp Koehn, Alexandre Mourachko, Christophe Ropers, Safiyyah Saleem, Holger Schwenk, and Jeff Wang. 2022. No Language Left Behind: Scaling Human-Centered Machine Translation. ArXiv:2207.04672 [cs].

Nohil Park, Joonsuk Park, Kang Min Yoo, and Sungroh Yoon. 2023. On the Analysis of Cross-Lingual Prompt Tuning for Decoder-based Multilingual Model. ArXiv:2311.07820 [cs].

Fred Philippy, Siwen Guo, and Shohreh Haddadan. 2023. Identifying the Correlation Between Language Distance and Cross-Lingual Transfer in a Multilingual Representation Space. In *Proceedings of the 5th Workshop on Research in Computational Linguistic Typology and Multilingual NLP*, pages 22–29, Dubrovnik, Croatia. Association for Computational Linguistics.

Anastasiia Razdaibiedina, Yuning Mao, Madian Khabsa, Mike Lewis, Rui Hou, Jimmy Ba, and Amjad Almahairi. 2023. Residual Prompt Tuning: improving prompt tuning with residual reparameterization. In *Findings of the Association for Computational Linguistics: ACL 2023*, pages 6740–6757, Toronto, Canada. Association for Computational Linguistics.

Teven Le Scao, Angela Fan, Christopher Akiki, Ellie Pavlick, Suzana Ilic, Daniel Hesslow, Roman Castagné, Alexandra Sasha Luccioni, François Yvon, Matthias Gallé, Jonathan Tow, Alexander M. Rush, Stella Biderman, Albert Webson, Pawan Sasanka Ammanamanchi, Thomas Wang, Benoît Sagot, Niklas Muennighoff, Albert Villanova del Moral, Olatunji Ruwase, Rachel Bawden, Stas Bekman, Angelina McMillan-Major, Iz Beltagy, Huu Nguyen, Lucile Saulnier, Samson Tan, Pedro Ortiz Suarez, Victor Sanh, Hugo Laurençon, Yacine Jernite, Julien Launay, Margaret Mitchell, Colin Raffel, Aaron Gokaslan, Adi Simhi, Aitor Soroa, Alham Fikri Aji, Amit Alfassy, Anna Rogers, Ariel Kreisberg Nitzav, Canwen Xu, Chenghao Mou, Chris Emezue, Christopher Klamm, Colin Leong, Daniel van Strien, David Ifeoluwa Adelani, and et al. 2022. BLOOM: A 176B-Parameter Open-Access Multilingual Language Model. *CoRR*, abs/2211.05100. ArXiv: 2211.05100.

Lifu Tu, Caiming Xiong, and Yingbo Zhou. 2022. Prompt-Tuning Can Be Much Better Than Fine-Tuning on Cross-lingual Understanding With Multilingual Language Models. In *Findings of the Association for Computational Linguistics: EMNLP 2022*, pages 5478–5485, Abu Dhabi, United Arab Emirates. Association for Computational Linguistics.

Tu Vu, Aditya Barua, Brian Lester, Daniel Cer, Mohit Iyyer, and Noah Constant. 2022. Overcoming Catastrophic Forgetting in Zero-Shot Cross-Lingual Generation. In *Proceedings of the 2022 Conference on Empirical Methods in Natural Language Processing*, pages 9279–9300, Abu Dhabi, United Arab Emirates. Association for Computational Linguistics.

Thomas Wolf, Lysandre Debut, Victor Sanh, Julien Chaumond, Clement Delangue, Anthony Moi, Pierric Cistac, Tim Rault, Remi Louf, Morgan Funtowicz, Joe Davison, Sam Shleifer, Patrick von Platen, Clara Ma, Yacine Jernite, Julien Plu, Canwen Xu, Teven Le Scao, Sylvain Gugger, Mariama Drame, Quentin Lhoest, and Alexander Rush. 2020. Transformers: State-of-the-Art Natural Language Processing. In *Proceedings of the 2020 Conference on Empirical Methods in Natural Language Processing: System Demonstrations*, pages 38–45, Online. Association for Computational Linguistics.

Mengjie Zhao and Hinrich Schütze. 2021. Discrete and Soft Prompting for Multilingual Models. In *Proceedings of the 2021 Conference on Empirical Methods in Natural Language Processing*, pages 8547–8555, Online and Punta Cana, Dominican Republic. Association for Computational Linguistics.

A Reproducibility

We provide the code used for our experiments here: https://github.com/fredxlpy/cross_lingual_prompt_tuning.

A.1 Dataset

Our experiments are based on the SIB-200 dataset (Adelani et al., 2023). The dataset is based on the FLORES-200 benchmark (NLLB Team et al., 2022), and consists of 701 training, 99 validation and 204 test samples in each of the 203 languages. The task is to classify each sample into one of the 7 potential categories: `science/technology`, `travel`, `politics`, `sports`, `health`, `entertainment`, and `geography`.

A.2 Models

We provide additional information about the models used in our study in Table 2.

Model	Layers	Parameters	Hidden size	Vocab size
BLOOM-560M	24	560M	1.024	250.880
BLOOM-1.1B		1.1B	1.536	
XGLM-564M		564M	1.024	256.008
XGLM-1.7B		1.7B	2.048	

Table 2: Technical details of the models used in our study.

A.3 Technical Details

		Batch size	Learning rate	Prompt length
w/ MF	XGLM 564M	8	0.1	10
	XGLM 1.7B			
	BLOOM 560M			5
	BLOOM 1.1B			10
w/o MF	XGLM 564M	8	5e-6	10
	XGLM 1.7B			
	BLOOM 560M		1e-6	5
	BLOOM 1.1B			10

Table 3: Hyperparameters used in all of our experiments.

We conducted all of our experiments using the *Transformers* library (Wolf et al., 2020). In a k-shot setting, we fine-tune on k samples per class from the English train set and use $\frac{k}{4}$ samples per class for validation. We train all models and prompts for 20 epochs and select the best checkpoint on the development set. The different hyperparameters used in our experiments are provided in Table 3.

A.4 Soft Prompt

We follow the approach of Lester et al. (2021) and freeze all model parameters and only fine-tune the soft prompt.

In order to map the tokens predicted by the model to the respective class, we define a verbalizer $F : T \rightarrow C$, where $T = \{t_1, \ldots, t_K\}$ is a subset of the model's vocabulary V and $C = \{1, \ldots, K\}$ are the respective classes.

We append a prompt $p = \{p_1, \ldots, p_m\}$ to an input sequence $x = \{x_1, \ldots, x_n\}$ and pass $\{x_1, \ldots, x_n, p_1, \ldots, p_m\}$ through the autoregressive language model which outputs the logits for the next token in the input sequence $\{l_1, \ldots, l_{|V|}\}$.

The predicted token is then $F\left(argmax_{i \in T} l_i\right)$

A.5 Computing Resources

We conduct all our experiments on 4 A100 40GB GPUs, using 4 different random seeds, in parallel. All experiments could be run in a few hours.

B Language Distance Metrics

We consider six types of lang2vec[2] (Littell et al., 2017) distances:

- **Syntactic Distance** (SYN) captures the similarity of syntactic structures across languages. It is computed as the cosine distance between syntax feature vectors, which are derived from the World Atlas of Language Structures[3] (WALS) (Dryer and Haspelmath, 2013), Syntactic Structures of World Languages[4] (SSWL) (Collins and Kayne, 2011) and Ethnologue[5] (Lewis et al., 2015).

- **Geographic Distance** (GEO) reflects the spatial proximity of languages. It is calculated as the shortest distance between two languages on the surface of the earth's sphere (i.e., orthodromic distance).

- **Inventory Distance** (INV) measures the difference in sound inventories across languages. It is computed as the cosine distance between inventory feature vectors, which are obtained

[2] `https://github.com/antonisa/lang2vec`
[3] `https://wals.info`
[4] `http://sswl.railsplayground.net/`
[5] `https://www.ethnologue.com/`

from the PHOIBLE[6] database (Moran et al., 2019).

- **Genetic Distance** (GEN) indicates the historical relatedness of languages. It is based on the Glottolog[7] (Hammarström et al., 2015) tree of language families and is obtained by computing the distance between two languages in the tree.
- **Phonological Distance** (PHON) captures the similarity of sound patterns across languages. It is computed as the cosine distance between phonological feature vectors, which are sourced from WALS and Ethnologue.
- **Featural Distance** (FEA) is the cosine distance between feature vectors from a combination of the 5 above-listed linguistic features.

The values for each distance type range from 0 to 1, where 0 indicates the minimum distance and 1 indicates the maximum distance.

C Prompt Reparameterization

We follow the residual reparameterization method of Razdaibiedina et al. (2023) to examine the impact of soft prompt reparameterization. This method employs a multi-layer perceptron (MLP) architecture for the reparameterization network, which consists of a *down-projection* layer and an *up-projection* layer with parameter $W_{down} \in \mathbb{R}^{d \times m}$ and $W_{up} \in \mathbb{R}^{m \times d}$ respectively, where d denotes the model embedding size and m denotes the hidden representation dimension between both layers (*bottleneck size*). A ReLU layer is applied to the hidden representation, and a normalization layer is applied to the output of the *up-projection* layer before summing it with the initial input embedding via a residual connection. We fine-tune the soft prompt and its reparameterization network with a bottleneck size of 500 for BLOOM-560M and 200 for XGLM-564M and report the impact of reparameterization across all target languages in Figure 5. Except for the reparameterization, we adopt the same implementation settings as described in Section 3.

D Full Results

The full results discussed in Section 4 are provided in Table 4.

[6]https://phoible.org/
[7]https://glottolog.org

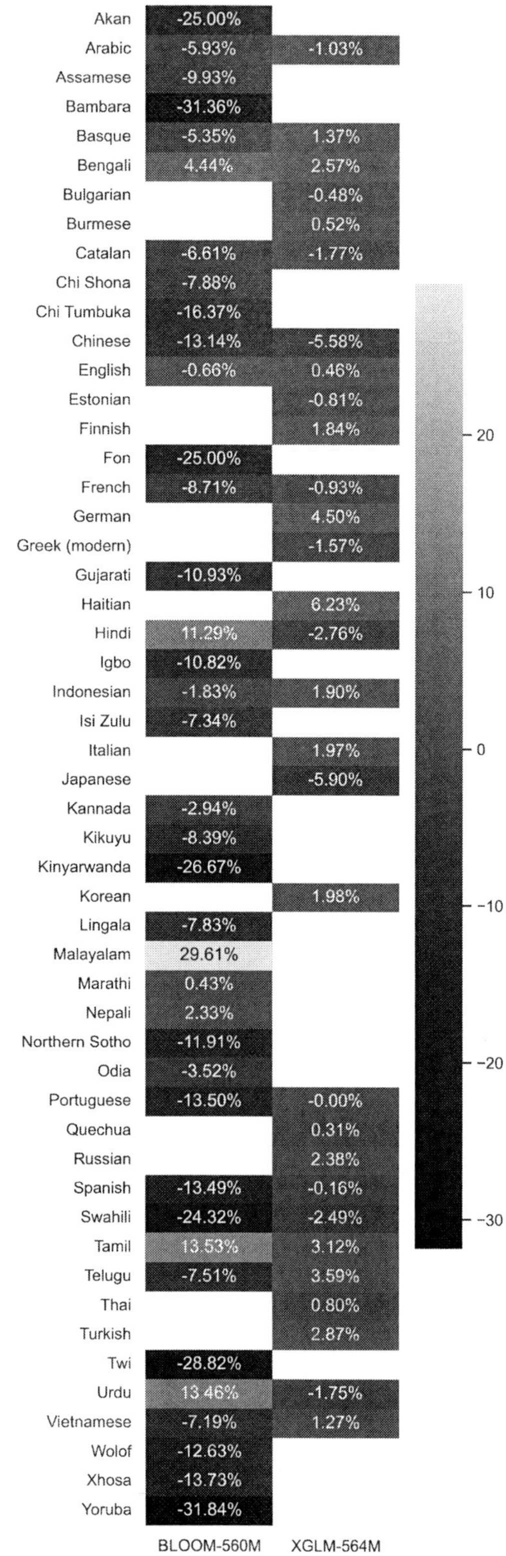

Figure 5: Impact of reparameterization (expressed in %) on the cross-lingual transfer performance of BLOOM-560M and XGLM-564M for different target languages.

Language	BLOOM-560M w/o MF	BLOOM-560M w/ MF	BLOOM-1.1B w/o MF	BLOOM-1.1B w/ MF	XGLM-564M w/o MF	XGLM-564M w/ MF	XGLM-1.7B w/o MF	XGLM-1.7B w/ MF
Akan	22,18$_{9,67}$	**34,80$_{6,33}$**	19,36$_{6,52}$	**35,05$_{0,85}$**	-	-	-	-
Arabic	55,51$_{3,56}$	**70,22$_{1,62}$**	42,03$_{11,9}$	**63,48$_{3,50}$**	57,60$_{3,34}$	**71,69$_{1,89}$**	74,75$_{1,67}$	**78,68$_{5,49}$**
Assamese	27,45$_{7,99}$	**37,01$_{4,85}$**	29,41$_{9,66}$	**53,06$_{4,92}$**	-	-	-	-
Bambara	16,67$_{3,63}$	**26,96$_{8,74}$**	17,03$_{5,94}$	**29,17$_{3,68}$**	-	-	-	-
Basque	43,50$_{12,5}$	**61,89$_{1,90}$**	38,73$_{7,69}$	**63,97$_{13,0}$**	67,40$_{1,30}$	**71,32$_{2,70}$**	71,08$_{3,07}$	**72,43$_{6,64}$**
Bengali	56,62$_{4,48}$	**60,78$_{2,41}$**	46,69$_{12,2}$	**71,81$_{2,90}$**	68,14$_{3,51}$	**71,45$_{4,24}$**	71,57$_{3,05}$	**76,23$_{5,22}$**
Bulgarian	-	-	-	-	72,79$_{5,13}$	**77,33$_{2,45}$**	78,92$_{2,40}$	**81,37$_{4,33}$**
Burmese	-	-	-	-	63,60$_{6,06}$	**71,20$_{3,38}$**	72,67$_{3,03}$	**73,41$_{7,79}$**
Catalan	63,48$_{13,1}$	**72,30$_{2,28}$**	48,77$_{7,93}$	**73,77$_{4,03}$**	68,50$_{7,52}$	**76,35$_{3,03}$**	77,33$_{4,01}$	**79,04$_{4,13}$**
Chi Shona	19,98$_{4,79}$	**24,88$_{2,67}$**	17,89$_{5,69}$	**31,00$_{3,95}$**	-	-	-	-
Chi Tumbuka	20,34$_{4,54}$	**27,70$_{2,55}$**	18,14$_{4,95}$	**33,70$_{4,62}$**	-	-	-	-
Chinese	60,54$_{11,1}$	**73,65$_{6,47}$**	47,30$_{13,9}$	**72,43$_{3,36}$**	59,93$_{8,33}$	**79,04$_{1,85}$**	77,94$_{5,08}$	**81,74$_{4,28}$**
English	**75,00$_{5,87}$**	74,63$_{2,09}$	69,36$_{2,67}$	**75,12$_{2,90}$**	78,68$_{1,67}$	**79,90$_{2,62}$**	80,88$_{2,94}$	**82,84$_{5,41}$**
Estonian	-	-	-	-	72,30$_{3,24}$	**75,86$_{3,13}$**	76,35$_{1,76}$	**81,13$_{5,78}$**
Finnish	-	-	-	-	76,72$_{1,81}$	**79,90$_{1,44}$**	79,78$_{1,76}$	**82,35$_{5,92}$**
Fon	19,36$_{10,0}$	**25,49$_{7,88}$**	13,97$_{3,98}$	**26,84$_{5,51}$**	-	-	-	-
French	69,61$_{6,52}$	**73,16$_{1,89}$**	57,23$_{6,29}$	**72,92$_{5,51}$**	71,94$_{4,26}$	**79,29$_{2,98}$**	79,04$_{5,48}$	**79,90$_{2,80}$**
German	-	-	-	-	71,57$_{7,19}$	**76,23$_{4,67}$**	81,62$_{5,04}$	81,62$_{5,79}$
Greek (modern)	-	-	-	-	73,90$_{3,47}$	**78,19$_{2,93}$**	80,27$_{2,70}$	**82,97$_{5,11}$**
Gujarati	**41,79$_{7,92}$**	37,01$_{9,35}$	27,08$_{7,85}$	**54,29$_{10,3}$**	-	-	-	-
Haitian	-	-	-	-	65,44$_{1,30}$	**68,87$_{2,55}$**	74,39$_{1,72}$	**74,75$_{6,70}$**
Hindi	42,52$_{4,28}$	**45,59$_{4,47}$**	50,12$_{10,0}$	**64,95$_{2,85}$**	74,14$_{3,28}$	**75,37$_{2,41}$**	75,74$_{2,95}$	**78,19$_{4,88}$**
Igbo	18,50$_{1,57}$	**23,77$_{6,42}$**	15,20$_{4,85}$	**27,70$_{4,57}$**	-	-	-	-
Indonesian	49,26$_{2,55}$	**66,91$_{1,86}$**	49,14$_{11,9}$	**68,75$_{3,38}$**	73,90$_{1,29}$	**77,57$_{2,45}$**	77,21$_{2,48}$	**79,90$_{5,34}$**
Isi Zulu	19,24$_{6,01}$	**21,69$_{2,72}$**	15,69$_{5,98}$	**29,66$_{2,48}$**	-	-	-	-
Italian	-	-	-	-	73,41$_{4,82}$	**74,75$_{1,52}$**	78,43$_{4,95}$	**80,02$_{5,52}$**
Japanese	-	-	-	-	54,29$_{5,98}$	**76,84$_{3,89}$**	**80,64$_{1,47}$**	77,94$_{4,65}$
Kannada	22,30$_{8,24}$	**25,00$_{8,46}$**	22,92$_{3,85}$	**55,76$_{7,93}$**	-	-	-	-
Kikuyu	28,19$_{8,36}$	**35,05$_{2,42}$**	19,49$_{4,44}$	**33,70$_{3,81}$**	-	-	-	-
Kinyarwanda	19,00$_{3,21}$	**25,74$_{6,26}$**	15,69$_{3,80}$	**30,39$_{4,33}$**	-	-	-	-
Korean	-	-	-	-	73,77$_{1,67}$	**74,26$_{2,28}$**	74,75$_{4,46}$	**77,45$_{5,41}$**
Lingala	23,90$_{3,85}$	**28,19$_{4,74}$**	21,69$_{8,43}$	**36,15$_{3,29}$**	-	-	-	-
Malayalam	**23,53$_{11,1}$**	21,94$_{7,56}$	30,39$_{9,95}$	**59,93$_{4,17}$**	-	-	-	-
Marathi	**34,68$_{11,1}$**	28,31$_{5,83}$	29,78$_{6,21}$	**60,05$_{4,41}$**	-	-	-	-
Nepali	30,15$_{6,99}$	**42,03$_{6,95}$**	36,76$_{13,3}$	**67,03$_{6,25}$**	-	-	-	-
Northern Sotho	20,59$_{6,62}$	**28,80$_{0,47}$**	18,38$_{4,09}$	**33,82$_{2,40}$**	-	-	-	-
Odia	**34,80$_{7,64}$**	31,37$_{6,62}$	25,00$_{5,25}$	**47,06$_{9,22}$**	-	-	-	-
Portuguese	66,67$_{5,02}$	**75,37$_{3,19}$**	53,19$_{5,69}$	**73,77$_{2,17}$**	74,26$_{1,90}$	**79,53$_{1,09}$**	80,15$_{1,98}$	**82,48$_{3,95}$**
Quechua	-	-	-	-	35,66$_{8,69}$	**39,71$_{2,23}$**	49,88$_{4,84}$	**51,59$_{6,37}$**
Russian	-	-	-	-	76,96$_{3,23}$	**77,21$_{1,98}$**	78,19$_{3,43}$	**80,27$_{4,30}$**
Spanish	63,36$_{8,94}$	**72,67$_{0,47}$**	46,69$_{9,79}$	**73,65$_{5,11}$**	71,45$_{0,74}$	**76,47$_{2,30}$**	77,33$_{3,63}$	**79,78$_{4,84}$**
Swahili	35,05$_{7,95}$	**49,88$_{6,02}$**	25,12$_{6,22}$	**49,75$_{7,40}$**	61,40$_{8,61}$	**69,00$_{2,84}$**	**73,77$_{2,45}$**	72,79$_{7,91}$
Tamil	44,85$_{9,58}$	**50,74$_{4,09}$**	34,44$_{13,1}$	**67,40$_{4,71}$**	68,75$_{5,68}$	**70,59$_{2,12}$**	73,90$_{1,01}$	**75,86$_{7,91}$**
Telugu	24,51$_{3,94}$	**31,00$_{6,71}$**	26,96$_{1,20}$	**66,05$_{7,13}$**	62,75$_{3,33}$	**68,26$_{5,15}$**	74,14$_{3,76}$	**76,23$_{6,46}$**
Thai	-	-	-	-	67,77$_{6,42}$	**76,35$_{1,16}$**	**79,53$_{1,72}$**	77,33$_{5,02}$
Turkish	-	-	-	-	73,16$_{2,84}$	**76,96$_{3,18}$**	74,63$_{4,30}$	**79,17$_{5,89}$**
Twi	23,41$_{9,5}$	**35,29$_{6,64}$**	18,75$_{6,83}$	**36,52$_{3,32}$**	-	-	-	-
Urdu	42,28$_{6,67}$	**44,61$_{8,95}$**	31,74$_{8,12}$	**48,41$_{9,35}$**	54,90$_{8,37}$	**70,10$_{2,86}$**	70,10$_{3,12}$	**75,25$_{5,69}$**
Vietnamese	46,08$_{19,4}$	**68,14$_{7,21}$**	43,87$_{7,49}$	**64,58$_{3,76}$**	70,71$_{3,06}$	**76,96$_{3,18}$**	78,31$_{3,63}$	**79,90$_{7,30}$**
Wolof	25,49$_{7,88}$	**34,93$_{4,17}$**	21,81$_{9,77}$	**41,42$_{4,64}$**	-	-	-	-
Xhosa	21,94$_{7,35}$	**28,55$_{1,23}$**	15,32$_{5,51}$	**32,23$_{6,14}$**	-	-	-	-
Yoruba	13,36$_{1,62}$	**21,94$_{9,49}$**	16,30$_{2,28}$	**33,21$_{4,76}$**	-	-	-	-

Table 4: Cross-lingual transfer results, reported as accuracy, along with standard deviation across 4 runs, after 8-shot soft prompt tuning (SPT) in English, with and without model freezing (MF).

Modular Adaptation of Multilingual Encoders to Written Swiss German Dialect

Jannis Vamvas **Noëmi Aepli** **Rico Sennrich**
Department of Computational Linguistics, University of Zurich
{vamvas,naepli,sennrich}@cl.uzh.ch

Abstract

Creating neural text encoders for written Swiss German is challenging due to a dearth of training data combined with dialectal variation. In this paper, we build on several existing multilingual encoders and adapt them to Swiss German using continued pre-training. Evaluation on three diverse downstream tasks shows that simply adding a Swiss German adapter to a modular encoder achieves 97.5% of fully monolithic adaptation performance. We further find that for the task of retrieving Swiss German sentences given Standard German queries, adapting a character-level model is more effective than the other adaptation strategies. We release our code and the models trained for our experiments.[1]

1 Introduction

When applying natural language processing (NLP) techniques to languages with dialectal variation, two typical challenges are a lack of public training data as well as varying spelling conventions. In the case of Swiss German, which is spoken by around 5 million people and is often used for informal written communication in Switzerland, these factors make it more challenging to train a BERT-like text encoder for written text.

In this paper, we adapt pre-trained multilingual encoders to Swiss German using continued pre-training on a modest amount of Swiss German training data. We evaluate the approaches on part-of-speech (POS) tagging with zero-shot cross-lingual transfer from Standard German (Aepli and Sennrich, 2022), as well as dialect identification (Zampieri et al., 2019) and cross-lingual sentence retrieval based on a parallel Standard German–Swiss German test set (Aepli et al., 2023).

We find that depending on the multilingual encoder, continued pre-training leads to an average

	Monolithic	**Modular**
Subwords	XLM-R → Swiss German XLM-R	X-MOD/SwissBERT → Swiss German adapter
Characters	CANINE → Swiss German CANINE	X-MOD/SwissBERT → Swiss German character-level adapter

Table 1: Overview of the encoder models we release.

improvement of 10%–45% in average accuracy across the three downstream tasks. We then focus on comparing monolithic adaptation, where all the parameters of the encoder are updated during continued pre-training, to modular adaptation with language-specific modular components (*language adapters*; Pfeiffer et al., 2022). Even though modular adaptation only updates a fraction of the parameters, it is competitive to monolithic adaptation. Given these findings, we propose to extend the SwissBERT model (Vamvas et al., 2023), which was trained on Standard German and other languages, with a Swiss German adapter (Table 1).

We further hypothesize that the architecture of CANINE (Clark et al., 2022), a tokenization-free model that operates on characters, might be better suited to the highly variable spelling of Swiss German. Indeed, a CANINE model adapted to Swiss German excels on the retrieval tasks, while POS tagging works better with subwords.

Finally, we aim to combine the best of both worlds by integrating character-level down- and upsampling modules into a subword-based model and training a *character-level adapter* for Swiss German. However, this jointly modular and tokenization-free strategy underperforms the individual approaches. We hope that our findings can inform the development of modular approaches for other languages with dialectal variation.

[1] https://github.com/ZurichNLP/swiss-german-text-encoders

Proceedings of the 1st Workshop on Modular and Open Multilingual NLP (MOOMIN 2024), pages 16–23
March 21, 2024

2 Adaptation Scenario

Our goal is to train an encoder model for Swiss German (language code gsw) with limited training data. Since Standard German (language code de) is a closely related language, we focus on transfer learning from Standard German to Swiss German. We rely on pre-trained multilingual models that have already been trained on Standard German, and adapt them to Swiss German using continued pre-training.

Swiss German adaptation data For training on Swiss German, we use the SwissCrawl corpus (Linder et al., 2020), which contains 11M tokens of Swiss German text extracted from the web. The text in SwissCrawl exhibits some normalizations that eventual input text will not have, e.g., isolation of individual sentences, normalization of punctuation and emoji removal. To diversify the training data, we extend the pre-training dataset with a custom collection of 382k Swiss German tweets. In total, we use 18M tokens for pre-training on Swiss German. Both datasets were automatically mined and may contain some text in other languages.

Standard German data To promote transfer from Standard German to Swiss German later on, we include an equal part of Standard German data in the continued pre-training data. We use a sample of news articles retrieved from the Swissdox@LiRI database, comparable to the data the SwissBERT model has been trained on (Vamvas et al., 2023).

3 Monolithic Approaches

We evaluate a subword-based model and a character-based model, with and without continued pre-training on Swiss German. We call these models monolithic (non-modular), because the entire model is updated during continued pre-training.

3.1 XLM-R

We train XLM-R (Conneau et al., 2020) with masked language modeling (MLM). XLM-R was pre-trained on 100 languages, which include Standard German but not Swiss German.

3.2 CANINE

The CANINE model (Clark et al., 2022) was pre-trained on 104 languages, again including Standard German but excluding Swiss German. Unlike XLM-R, CANINE directly encodes character sequences and does not require a tokenizer at inference time. This is achieved by extending the standard transformer architecture with character down- and upsampling modules.

The *downsampling module* combines a single-layer blockwise transformer with strided convolution, which reduces the sequence length by a factor of $r = 4$, where r is a hyperparameter. As a consequence, the standard transformer does not see every character individually, but only sees downsampled positions. The *upsampling module*, which is needed for token-level tasks, mirrors the downsampling procedure and restores the original sequence length. We refer to Clark et al. (2022) for a detailed description of the architecture.

Clark et al. (2022) describe two alternative approaches for pre-training: CANINE-S, which uses a tokenizer to determine masked tokens and is similar to standard MLM, and CANINE-C, which is an autoregressive character loss. In our experiments, we use CANINE-S with the SwissBERT subword tokenizer to perform continued pre-training.

4 Modular Approaches

4.1 SwissBERT

We base our adapter experiments on SwissBERT (Vamvas et al., 2023), a variant of X-MOD (Pfeiffer et al., 2022) that includes language adapters for Standard German, French, Italian and Romansh. Compared to the original X-MOD model, which was trained with language adapters for 81 languages, SwissBERT has a custom SentencePiece vocabulary and word embeddings optimized for Switzerland-related text, and we assume that this is beneficial for continued pre-training on Swiss German.

4.2 Subword-level Adapter for SwissBERT

We add a Swiss German adapter to SwissBERT and freeze the parameters of the model except for the adapter modules during continued pre-training. We initialize the Swiss German adapter with the weights of the Standard German adapter and pre-train it on the Swiss German part of our dataset. During fine-tuning on downstream tasks, we freeze the adapters and update the remainder of the model.

For this approach, we only use the Swiss German part of our pre-training corpus for continued pre-training, and not Standard German, since the modular architecture is expected to allow for cross-lingual transfer without continued pre-training

	POS	GDI	Retrieval		Macro-Avg.
			GSW-BE	GSW-ZH	
XLM-R:					
– without continued pre-training	52.6±1.8	47.2±15.1	60.6	75.7	56.0
– with continued pre-training	<u>86.9±0.3</u>	62.1±0.8	91.1	96.0	<u>80.9</u>
CANINE:					
– without continued pre-training	46.7±1.3	59.0±0.6	92.8	94.8	66.5
– with continued pre-training	60.9±1.4	60.8±0.4	<u>96.4</u>	<u>96.9</u>	72.8
SwissBERT:					
– DE adapter without continued pre-training	64.8±2.0	61.3±0.5	66.1	82.2	66.7
– subword-level GSW adapter	83.2±0.3	62.0±0.4	82.9	92.4	77.6
– character-level GSW adapter	41.5±0.9	51.9±1.3	35.6	42.6	44.2

Table 2: Comparison of different models on three downstream tasks: part-of-speech (POS) tagging accuracy, German dialect identification (GDI) F1-score, and cross-lingual sentence retrieval accuracy. For the supervised tasks, we report the average and standard deviation across 5 fine-tuning runs. Underlined results indicate the best performance for a task.

on the source language. Table A4 provides an overview of the languages used for each approach.

4.3 Character-level Adapter for SwissBERT

Previous work has found that learning a custom subword segmentation and embeddings that are adapted to the vocabulary of the target language can improve performance (Wang et al., 2019; Pfeiffer et al., 2021; Vamvas et al., 2023). However, this limits the degree of modularity, and we thus investigate a tokenization-free approach as an alternative. In this experiment, we discard SwissBERT's subword embeddings when training the Swiss German adapter, and instead add the downsampling and upsampling modules of the CANINE architecture.[2]

Adding these modules results in exactly the same architecture as CANINE, except that we opt for byte embeddings instead of character hash embeddings. CANINE uses a hash embedding method that can map any Unicode code point to a fixed-size embedding. Since Standard German and Swiss German are mainly written in Latin script and there are limited training data, we forgo the hash embedding and learn UTF-8 byte embeddings instead.

Using the CANINE-S objective, we first pre-train the character modules on Standard German pre-training data. We then continue pre-training the adapters and the joint character modules on both languages, while freezing the rest of the model. During fine-tuning, we freeze the adapters and train the remainder, analogous to the subword-level experiment.

5 Evaluation

5.1 Part-of-Speech Tagging (POS)

Following Aepli and Sennrich (2022), we evaluate our models on POS tagging with zero-shot cross-lingual transfer from Standard German. To train the models, we use the German HDT Universal Dependencies Treebank (Borges Völker et al., 2019) and test on a dataset introduced by Hollenstein and Aepli (2014). We report accuracy across the 54 STTS tags (Schiller et al., 1999).[3] We rely on the provided word segmentation and label the first token (subword/character/byte) of each word.

5.2 German Dialect Identification (GDI)

The GDI task (Zampieri et al., 2019) is based on transcripts of the ArchiMob corpus of spoken Swiss German (Samardžić et al., 2016). This dataset contains four dialects, namely, Bern, Basel, Lucerne, and Zurich regions, constituting four distinct classes. We report the weighted F1-score.

5.3 Sentence Retrieval

For evaluating cross-lingual sentence retrieval, we use human translations of the English `newstest2019` source dataset (Barrault et al., 2019) into different languages. Translations into

[2]We term this approach GLOBI (**G**ranular **Lo**calization of **Bi**directional Encoders).

[3]We mask the APPRART gold tag, which is not included in the training tag set, when calculating accuracy.

	POS	GDI	Retrieval		Macro-Avg.
			GSW-BE	GSW-ZH	
SwissBERT subword-level GSW adapter:					
– only updating the adapter weights	83.2±0.3	62.0±0.4	82.9	92.4	77.6 (97.5%)
– also updating the word embeddings	83.9±0.1	62.1±0.3	86.0	93.7	78.6 (98.7%)
– updating all the weights	85.7±0.3	63.1±0.3	86.6	93.4	79.6 (100%)

Table 3: Effect of modularity on continued pre-training: Only updating the adapter weights during continued pre-training achieves 97.5% of the accuracy of a monolithic baseline where we update all the parameters of SwissBERT.

Standard German are provided by NTREX-128 (Federmann et al., 2022); translations into Swiss German are provided by Aepli et al. (2023) for two regions, Bern (`gsw-be`) and Zurich (`gsw-zh`).

For both Swiss German test sets, we report the top-1 accuracy of retrieving the correct translation among all 1,997 translations, given the Standard German equivalent. Note that 100% accuracy is not attainable, since `newstest2019` has a small number of duplicate or near-duplicate sentences. Following an evaluation approach used for SwissBERT (Vamvas et al., 2023), we perform unsupervised retrieval with the BERTScore metric (Zhang et al., 2020). We average the hidden states across all encoder layers. In the case of the CANINE-style models, we use only the transformer layers that represent the downsampled positions.

6 Experimental Setup

Continued pre-training We combine Swiss German and Standard German training data with a 1:1 ratio. The resulting bilingual dataset contains 37M tokens in total, and we set aside 5% for validation (Table A6). We set the learning rate to 1e-4 and select the best checkpoint based on the validation loss out of 10 epochs; otherwise we use the default settings of Hugging Face transformer's MLM example script. We train the models on a Nvidia V100 GPU with 32GB of memory and adjust the batch size dynamically to fit the available memory. With the subword-based models, we set the sequence length to 512. With the CANINE-style models, we use the default downsampling rate of $r = 4$ and a sequence length of $r \times 512 = 2048$ tokens (characters or bytes).

Fine-tuning For the downstream tasks that involve fine-tuning (POS and GDI), we fine-tune the model with a learning rate of 2e-5 and a batch size of 16. We train for 10 epochs and select the best checkpoint based on the validation accuracy. We report average and standard deviation across 5 fine-tuning runs with different random seeds.

7 Results

Table 2 presents a comparison of the different models on the three downstream tasks. Continued pre-training is highly beneficial for written Swiss German, confirming previous work (Muller et al., 2021; Aepli and Sennrich, 2022; Aepli et al., 2023). This finding extends to the CANINE model, for which language-adaptive pre-training has not been tested before, to our knowledge.

The adapted CANINE shows state-of-the-art performance on the retrieval tasks. A simple ChrF baseline (Popović, 2015) achieves only 90.9% and 93.0% accuracy on the two retrieval tasks, and both the original and the adapted CANINE clearly surpass this baseline. However, the CANINE model has low accuracy on POS tagging, reflecting previous findings for named entity recognition (Clark et al., 2022). Future work could explore alternative strategies for token-level classification tasks.

While the monolithic XLM-R model performs best overall, we consider adding a subword-based Swiss German adapter to SwissBERT a competitive alternative, with the number of trainable parameters reduced by 95% (see Table A1 for a comparison of the model sizes). Table 3 confirms that restricting the continued pre-training to the adapter weights conserves most of the accuracy, compared to updating all the parameters of SwissBERT.

Finally, a character-level adapter, where character up- and downsampling modules are added to the model specifically for Swiss German, performs better than random but clearly worse than the standard approaches. This indicates that while the transformer layers of a subword-based model bear some similarity to the downsampled positions in the CANINE architecture, continued pre-training cannot completely bridge the gap between the two architectures. Future work could pre-train a modular character-level model from scratch to further improve adaptability to new languages and dialects, while taking into account more recent findings regarding the optimal design of character-level modules for text encoding (Tay et al., 2022; Cao, 2023).

8 Conclusion

We compared strategies for adapting multilingual encoders to Swiss German. We found that the monolithic approach of continued pre-training XLM-R is a strong baseline. Adding a Swiss German adapter to SwissBERT, a model with a modular architecture, is a viable alternative. Finally, adapting CANINE on Swiss German works well for cross-lingual retrieval. The four Swiss German encoder models we trained for our experiments will be made available to the research community.

Limitations

Differences between the pre-trained models make a fair comparison more difficult. The encoder models we compare have originally been pre-trained with different data and hyperparameters (but never on Swiss German). They also differ in their number of parameters and vocabulary sizes, as detailed in Table A1. Furthermore, we use a single, standard set of hyperparameters for pre-training and for evaluation, respectively. Optimizing these hyperparameters for each model individually could lead to further improvements.

Finally, the evaluation results show that it is challenging to perform GDI classification purely based on written text, as previously discussed by Zampieri et al. (2017). In interpreting the results, we focus mainly on the other two tasks, but still report results for GDI to provide a complete picture.

Acknowledgements

This work was funded by the Swiss National Science Foundation (project nos. 213976 and 191934). We thank Stefan Langer for helpful advice on collecting the Swiss German tweet dataset, and Chantal Amrhein for the provision of test data. For this publication, use was made of media data made available via Swissdox@LiRI by the Linguistic Research Infrastructure of the University of Zurich (see `https://t.uzh.ch/1hI` for more information).

References

Noëmi Aepli, Chantal Amrhein, Florian Schottmann, and Rico Sennrich. 2023. A benchmark for evaluating machine translation metrics on dialects without standard orthography. In *Proceedings of the Eighth Conference on Machine Translation*, pages 1045–1065, Singapore. Association for Computational Linguistics.

Noëmi Aepli and Rico Sennrich. 2022. Improving zero-shot cross-lingual transfer between closely related languages by injecting character-level noise. In *Findings of the Association for Computational Linguistics: ACL 2022*, pages 4074–4083, Dublin, Ireland. Association for Computational Linguistics.

Loïc Barrault, Ondřej Bojar, Marta R. Costa-jussà, Christian Federmann, Mark Fishel, Yvette Graham, Barry Haddow, Matthias Huck, Philipp Koehn, Shervin Malmasi, Christof Monz, Mathias Müller, Santanu Pal, Matt Post, and Marcos Zampieri. 2019. Findings of the 2019 conference on machine translation (WMT19). In *Proceedings of the Fourth Conference on Machine Translation (Volume 2: Shared Task Papers, Day 1)*, pages 1–61, Florence, Italy. Association for Computational Linguistics.

Emanuel Borges Völker, Maximilian Wendt, Felix Hennig, and Arne Köhn. 2019. HDT-UD: A very large Universal Dependencies treebank for German. In *Proceedings of the Third Workshop on Universal Dependencies (UDW, SyntaxFest 2019)*, pages 46–57, Paris, France. Association for Computational Linguistics.

Kris Cao. 2023. What is the best recipe for character-level encoder-only modelling? In *Proceedings of the 61st Annual Meeting of the Association for Computational Linguistics (Volume 1: Long Papers)*, pages 5924–5938, Toronto, Canada. Association for Computational Linguistics.

Jonathan H. Clark, Dan Garrette, Iulia Turc, and John Wieting. 2022. Canine: Pre-training an efficient tokenization-free encoder for language representation. *Transactions of the Association for Computational Linguistics*, 10:73–91.

Alexis Conneau, Kartikay Khandelwal, Naman Goyal, Vishrav Chaudhary, Guillaume Wenzek, Francisco Guzmán, Edouard Grave, Myle Ott, Luke Zettlemoyer, and Veselin Stoyanov. 2020. Unsupervised cross-lingual representation learning at scale. In *Proceedings of the 58th Annual Meeting of the Association for Computational Linguistics*, pages 8440–8451, Online. Association for Computational Linguistics.

Christian Federmann, Tom Kocmi, and Ying Xin. 2022. NTREX-128 – news test references for MT evaluation of 128 languages. In *Proceedings of the First Workshop on Scaling Up Multilingual Evaluation*, pages 21–24, Online. Association for Computational Linguistics.

Nora Hollenstein and Noëmi Aepli. 2014. Compilation of a Swiss German dialect corpus and its application to PoS tagging. In *Proceedings of the First Workshop on Applying NLP Tools to Similar Languages, Varieties and Dialects*, pages 85–94, Dublin, Ireland. Association for Computational Linguistics and Dublin City University.

Taku Kudo and John Richardson. 2018. SentencePiece: A simple and language independent subword tokenizer and detokenizer for neural text processing. In *Proceedings of the 2018 Conference on Empirical Methods in Natural Language Processing: System Demonstrations*, pages 66–71, Brussels, Belgium. Association for Computational Linguistics.

Lucy Linder, Michael Jungo, Jean Hennebert, Claudiu Cristian Musat, and Andreas Fischer. 2020. Automatic creation of text corpora for low-resource languages from the Internet: The case of Swiss German. In *Proceedings of the Twelfth Language Resources and Evaluation Conference*, pages 2706–2711, Marseille, France. European Language Resources Association.

Benjamin Muller, Antonios Anastasopoulos, Benoît Sagot, and Djamé Seddah. 2021. When being unseen from mBERT is just the beginning: Handling new languages with multilingual language models. In *Proceedings of the 2021 Conference of the North American Chapter of the Association for Computational Linguistics: Human Language Technologies*, pages 448–462, Online. Association for Computational Linguistics.

Jonas Pfeiffer, Naman Goyal, Xi Lin, Xian Li, James Cross, Sebastian Riedel, and Mikel Artetxe. 2022. Lifting the curse of multilinguality by pre-training modular transformers. In *Proceedings of the 2022 Conference of the North American Chapter of the Association for Computational Linguistics: Human Language Technologies*, pages 3479–3495, Seattle, United States. Association for Computational Linguistics.

Jonas Pfeiffer, Ivan Vulić, Iryna Gurevych, and Sebastian Ruder. 2021. UNKs everywhere: Adapting multilingual language models to new scripts. In *Proceedings of the 2021 Conference on Empirical Methods in Natural Language Processing*, pages 10186–10203, Online and Punta Cana, Dominican Republic. Association for Computational Linguistics.

Maja Popović. 2015. chrF: character n-gram F-score for automatic MT evaluation. In *Proceedings of the Tenth Workshop on Statistical Machine Translation*, pages 392–395, Lisbon, Portugal. Association for Computational Linguistics.

Tanja Samardžić, Yves Scherrer, and Elvira Glaser. 2016. ArchiMob - a corpus of spoken Swiss German. In *Proceedings of the Tenth International Conference on Language Resources and Evaluation (LREC'16)*, pages 4061–4066, Portorož, Slovenia. European Language Resources Association (ELRA).

Anne Schiller, Simone Teufel, Christine Stöckert, and Christine Thielen. 1999. Guidelines für das Tagging deutscher Textkorpora mit STTS.

Yi Tay, Vinh Q. Tran, Sebastian Ruder, Jai Gupta, Hyung Won Chung, Dara Bahri, Zhen Qin, Simon Baumgartner, Cong Yu, and Donald Metzler. 2022. Charformer: Fast character transformers via gradient-based subword tokenization. In *International Conference on Learning Representations*.

Jannis Vamvas, Johannes Graën, and Rico Sennrich. 2023. SwissBERT: The multilingual language model for Switzerland. In *Proceedings of the 8th edition of the Swiss Text Analytics Conference*, pages 54–69, Neuchatel, Switzerland. Association for Computational Linguistics.

Hai Wang, Dian Yu, Kai Sun, Jianshu Chen, and Dong Yu. 2019. Improving pre-trained multilingual model with vocabulary expansion. In *Proceedings of the 23rd Conference on Computational Natural Language Learning (CoNLL)*, pages 316–327, Hong Kong, China. Association for Computational Linguistics.

Marcos Zampieri, Shervin Malmasi, Nikola Ljubešić, Preslav Nakov, Ahmed Ali, Jörg Tiedemann, Yves Scherrer, and Noëmi Aepli. 2017. Findings of the VarDial evaluation campaign 2017. In *Proceedings of the Fourth Workshop on NLP for Similar Languages, Varieties and Dialects (VarDial)*, pages 1–15, Valencia, Spain. Association for Computational Linguistics.

Marcos Zampieri, Shervin Malmasi, Yves Scherrer, Tanja Samardžić, Francis Tyers, Miikka Silfverberg, Natalia Klyueva, Tung-Le Pan, Chu-Ren Huang, Radu Tudor Ionescu, Andrei M. Butnaru, and Tommi Jauhiainen. 2019. A report on the third VarDial evaluation campaign. In *Proceedings of the Sixth Workshop on NLP for Similar Languages, Varieties and Dialects*, pages 1–16, Ann Arbor, Michigan. Association for Computational Linguistics.

Tianyi Zhang, Varsha Kishore, Felix Wu, Kilian Q. Weinberger, and Yoav Artzi. 2020. BERTScore: Evaluating text generation with BERT. In *International Conference on Learning Representations*.

A List of Encoder Models

Model	Total parameters	Trained	Vocabulary size	URLs (original→adapted)
XLM-R	278M	278M	250,002	↗ → ↗
CANINE	132M†	132M	-	↗ → ↗
SwissBERT				
– subword-level adaptation	139M‡	8M	50,262	↗ → ↗
– character-level adaptation	123M‡	38M‡	261	↗ → ↗

Table A1: The main encoders trained in this work. † Figure does not include the CANINE-S output embeddings, which can be discarded after pre-training. ‡ Figure includes two adapters (Swiss German and Standard German).

B Ablation Study: Custom Subword Vocabulary

	POS	GDI	Retrieval		Macro-Avg.
			GSW-BE	GSW-ZH	
XLM-R:					
– XLM-R vocabulary	86.9±0.3	62.1±0.8	91.1	96.0	80.9
– custom GSW vocabulary	60.3±0.4	60.0±0.6	64.2	79.9	64.1
SwissBERT subword-level GSW adapter†:					
– SwissBERT vocabulary	83.9±0.1	62.1±0.3	86.0	93.7	78.6
– custom GSW vocabulary	23.7±2.3	56.9±0.6	65.6	77.3	50.7
CANINE:					
– CANINE-S with SwissBERT vocabulary	60.9±1.4	60.8±0.4	96.4	96.9	72.8
– CANINE-S with custom GSW vocabulary	57.8±1.2	62.1±0.6	95.6	96.3	71.9
SwissBERT character-level GSW adapter:					
– CANINE-S with SwissBERT vocabulary	41.5±0.9	51.9±1.3	35.6	42.6	44.2
– CANINE-S with custom GSW vocabulary	40.6±1.2	11.0±1.9	28.7	38.4	28.4

Table A2: In an ablation experiment, we create a custom subword vocabulary for our continued pre-training dataset using SentencePiece (Kudo and Richardson, 2018). For the subword-based models, we train a new embedding matrix while initializing it with lexically overlapping embeddings from the original model. Using the custom vocabulary for Swiss German decreases performance on all downstream tasks, probably due to the limited amount of training data. For the character-based models, we use the CANINE-S objective with the custom vocabulary. Surprisingly, the custom vocabulary decreases performance, possibly because it is less similar to the subword vocabulary originally used by Clark et al. (2022) to train CANINE-S. † In this experiment, we update the embedding weights of SwissBERT to enable a fair comparison.

Vocabulary	Vocabulary Size	Compression Ratio
XLM-R vocabulary	250,002	3.36
SwissBERT vocabulary	50,262	3.37
Custom GSW vocabulary	50,262	4.17

Table A3: Comparison of the SentencePiece vocabularies involved in the above ablation study. We report the compression ratio as the number of characters per subword token in a tokenized sample of our continued pre-training dataset.

C Model Training Details

Approach	Languages trained	Training samples per second
XLM-R continued pre-training	GSW + DE	88.9
CANINE continued pre-training	GSW + DE	149.6
SwissBERT character-level adapter	GSW + DE	127.1
SwissBERT subword-level adapter:		
– only updating the adapter weights	GSW	215.3
– also updating the word embeddings	GSW	202.4
– updating all the weights	GSW	225.9

Table A4: Empirical training speed in terms of training samples per second. Note that training speed is only comparable for models trained on the same languages, since the DE samples are longer than the GSW samples.

D Pre-training Datasets

Dataset	Language	Time Range	Examples	Tokens	URL
SwissCrawl (Linder et al., 2020)	GSW	until 2019	563,037	10,961,075	↗
Swiss German Tweets	GSW	2007–2018	381,654	7,259,477	-
Swissdox Sample	DE	2021	409,572	351,643,710	↗

Table A5: Details of the datasets from which we source data for continued pre-training.

Split	**Examples** (news articles / tweets / sentences)	Tokens
Training GSW	897,477	17,308,288
Training DE	20,140	17,459,689
Validation GSW	47,214	912,264
Validation DE	1,082	905,476

Table A6: Training and validation splits used for continued pre-training.

E Evaluation Datasets

Dataset	Examples	Tokens	Citation	URL
POS DE (train)	75,617	13,655,973	Borges Völker et al. (2019)	↗
POS DE (validation)	18,434	324,848	Borges Völker et al. (2019)	↗
POS GSW (test)	7,320	113,565	Hollenstein and Aepli (2014)	↗
GDI (train)	14,279	112,707	Zampieri et al. (2019)	-
GDI (validation)	4,530	33,579	Zampieri et al. (2019)	-
GDI (test)	4,743	42,699	Zampieri et al. (2019)	-
Retrieval DE	1,997	50,833	Federmann et al. (2022)	↗
Retrieval GSW-BE	1,997	53,119	Aepli et al. (2023)	↗
Retrieval GSW-ZH	1,997	54,501	Aepli et al. (2023)	↗

Table A7: Dataset statistics for the downstream tasks.

The Impact of Language Adapters in Cross-Lingual Transfer for NLU

Jenny Kunz*
Linköping University
jenny.kunz@liu.se

Oskar Holmström*
Linköping University
oskar.holmstrom@liu.se

Abstract

Modular deep learning has been proposed for the efficient adaption of pre-trained models to new tasks, domains and languages. In particular, combining language adapters with task adapters has shown potential where no supervised data exists for a language. In this paper, we explore the role of language adapters in zero-shot cross-lingual transfer for natural language understanding (NLU) benchmarks. We study the effect of including a target-language adapter in detailed ablation studies with two multilingual models and three multilingual datasets. Our results show that the effect of target-language adapters is highly inconsistent across tasks, languages and models. Retaining the source-language adapter instead often leads to an equivalent, and sometimes to a better, performance. Removing the language adapter after training has only a weak negative effect, indicating that the language adapters do not have a strong impact on the predictions.

1 Introduction

Adding smaller components to a large language model (LLM) that can be specifically targeted, trained, stacked and exchanged is becoming increasingly common (Pfeiffer et al., 2023). Particularly adapters (Houlsby et al., 2019) and LoRA (Hu et al., 2021) are widespread for the efficient adaption of LLMs. They often perform on par or better than fine-tuning the models' parameters while avoiding issues of interference such as catastrophic forgetting (McCloskey and Cohen, 1989; Ratcliff, 1990).

In this work, we focus on pre-trained target-language adapters for zero-shot cross-lingual transfer. Pfeiffer et al. (2020b) found that any cross-lingual transfer problem can be decomposed in language and task, and introduce a setup that combines task and language adapters, both independently trained on top of a pre-trained multilingual model. This setup is appealing particularly for low-resource and medium-resource languages that lack high-quality data for supervised training as it can be applied to unseen task-language combinations. However, how consistent the effect of the target-language adapter is has not been explored explicitly. In particular, it has not been explored how including target-language adapters compares to keeping the source-language adapter for the cross-lingual transfer. In addition, the detailed ablations by Pfeiffer et al. (2020b) focus on named entity recognition, while it remains unclear if similar results also hold for higher-level language understanding tasks. Therefore, we focus on three multilingual natural language understanding (NLU) benchmarks. We investigate the following questions:

RQ1. *How robust is the positive effect of adding a target-language adapter across languages, models and tasks?* To answer this question, we compare the performance with target-language adapters to other setups that keep the source-language adapter or that only include task adapters.

RQ2. *How much does the model rely on the effect of the language adapters?* We test this with a setup that leaves out the language adapter without substitution, and measure the performance drop.

RQ3. *Does the amount of source-language and target-language pre-training data in the base model affect the effect of the target-language adapter?* We compare the effect of target-language and source-language adapters conditioned on the languages' representation in the pre-training corpora.

Surprisingly, our extensive ablations show that instead of using the target-language adapter, we can often retain the source-language adapter that was

*Equal Contribution

Proceedings of the 1st Workshop on Modular and Open Multilingual NLP (MOOMIN 2024), pages 24–43
March 21, 2024 ©2024 Association for Computational Linguistics

used during training, or even leave out the language adapter after training with no negative (or even positive) effects on the models' performance. Even a setup that does not include language adapters at all is competitive and sometimes better. The results are however inconsistent across models, datasets and language pairs. We observe a higher benefit of target-language adapters for lower-resource target languages, but only for one out of four model-task combinations.

We conclude that the contribution of language adapters is less clear than we thought and that they do not play an interpretable role in the decision-making for language understanding tasks. However, they sometimes have a strong positive effect on the performance, making it worthwhile to test them in scenarios where they could be useful. We suggest putting more effort into understanding if there are interpretable properties of the base model, task, source language or target language that cause gains when using language adapters.

2 Related Work

Modular Deep Learning. Modular deep learning has gained attention with the primary goal of adapting pre-trained models to new tasks and languages efficiently, but also to avoid issues of interference such as catastrophic forgetting (McCloskey and Cohen, 1989; Ratcliff, 1990) and the curse of multilinguality (Conneau et al., 2020). Adapters (Houlsby et al., 2019) introduce a small number of additional parameters, which increases the inference overhead (Hu et al., 2021) but shows promising performance. For large-enough models (>3B parameters), language-specific adapters are even reported to outperform continued pre-training on unseen target languages (Yong et al., 2022). On the other hand, Ebrahimi and Kann (2021) report that for the XLM-R (Conneau et al., 2020) model, language adapters perform inferior to target-language fine-tuning. Crucially, post-hoc fine-tuning of adapters reportedly performs on par with including them in pre-training (Kim et al., 2021), which makes them particularly attractive where computational resources are limited.

Language Adapters. For language transfer with adapters, some work has focused on aggregating information from related languages, language families and genera. In the study by Lauscher et al. (2020), syntactic tasks rely heavily on language similarity, while it is less pronounced (though still existent) for semantic tasks. The UDapter framework (Üstün et al., 2020) integrates language adapters in a syntactic dependency parsing model, conditioned on typological features of the language. Faisal and Anastasopoulos (2022) adapt MLMs to unseen languages using hierarchical adapters inspired by phylogenetic trees. The tree hierarchy enables linguistically informed parameter sharing between related languages, leading to strong performance gains, especially for very low-resource languages and zero-shot transfer. This structured approach is apparently getting more consistent results than continued pre-training, where a diverse set of languages can top related languages (Fujinuma et al., 2022).

The MAD-X framework (Pfeiffer et al., 2020b) combines independently trained language and task adapters. Input embeddings are also processed by *invertible adapters*, whose inverse processes the output embeddings. They report successful cross-lingual transfer even for unseen combinations, making it possible to use models even where no annotated data exists for a language and even if the language was unseen during model pre-training. For cross-lingual transfer from a *monolingual* model, (Artetxe et al., 2020)'s results indicate some improvement using Houlsby-style language adapters over exchanging the token embeddings only for NLU tasks . However, Ebrahimi and Kann (2021) report that for languages unseen during pre-training, performing continued pre-training outperforms training language adapters and invertible adapters. He et al. (2021) explore task adapters (with no language adapters) for cross-lingual transfer on XLM-R and find that they perform better than fine-tuning, both on the full data and on low-resource setups. They hypothesize that adapters better maintain the target-language knowledge from pre-training as the original model's parameters are not changed. Pfeiffer et al. (2022) propose a framework that introduces language modularity at pre-training time, overcoming interference at no parametric cost.

3 Experimental Setup

In the following, we introduce the models, adapters, adapter training setups, ablation setups and datasets that we use for our ablation studies of language adapters. A link to our code including hyperparameters used to run our experiments will be published after the anonymity period. The code, including the hyperparameters used to run our experiments, is available at `https://github.com/oskarholmstrom/lang-adapters-impact`.

3.1 Model and Adapters

We use XLM-Roberta-base (XLM-R), trained on 100 languages (Conneau and Lample, 2019; Conneau et al., 2020), and multilingual BERT (mBERT), trained on 104 languages (Devlin et al., 2019). Most languages we test on are included in the pre-training of both models with the exception of Haitian Creole (ht) for XLM-R and Quechua (qu) for both models. We use pre-trained language adapters from AdapterHub (Pfeiffer et al., 2020a). We train task-specific Pfeiffer adapters using AdapterHub's associated *adapter-transformers* library[1]. Only task adapter parameters and classification heads are trained; language adapters and model parameters are kept frozen.

Adapter Setups. We train models with source-language adapters and evaluate them on the target language in three setups:

- *Target* replaces source-language adapters with target-language adapters at evaluation time.
- *Source* keeps the source-language adapters even at evaluation time.
- *None* leaves out the language adapter entirely at evaluation time (although still trained with source-language adapters).

To test if language adapters are beneficial at all, we include a fourth setup:

- In $None_{tr}$, models are both trained and evaluated without language adapters. Only task adapters are included in the models.

Pre-Training Data. For ablations that test the effect of the representation of the source- and target language in the pre-training corpus, we create a ranking. For XLM-R, we use the data on language representation given in the original paper (Conneau and Lample, 2019). mBERT is trained on Wikipedia data[2]. While no exact numbers or details on the dump are given, we estimate the size with the current number of articles for each language[3]. Wikipedia data was also used for the pre-training of the language adapters.

Lang.	XLM-R (#Tokens)	mBERT (#Articles)
Ar	2,869M	1.2M
De	10,297M	2.9M
El	4,285M	229K
En	55,608M	6.8M
Es	9,374M	1.9M
Et	843M	241K
Hi	1,715M	160K
Ht	not included	69K
Id	2,2704M	676K
Ja	530M	1.4M
Qu	not included	not included (24K)
Ru	23,408M	2.0M
Sw	275M	79K
Tr	2,736M	543K
Vi	24,757M	1,3M
Zh	259M+176M	1.4M

Table 1: Representation of languages in the pre-training corpora of the models. The mBERT data is approximated with the current number of Wikipedia articles. Quechua was not included in mBERT's pre-training. Wikipedia data was also used for the pre-training of the language adapters.

3.2 Data Sets

We evaluate language adapters on three natural language understanding and commonsense reasoning data sets. All data sets include human translations from the English original into several diverse languages, and are balanced with respect to the different labels. XCOPA is the only of the three data sets that was also included in the original MAD-X evaluation (Pfeiffer et al., 2020b).

PAWS-X. English PAWS (Zhang et al., 2019) is a paraphrase detection data set. Specifically, the task is to classify if a pair of sentences is a paraphrase or not. PAWS includes 108,463 paraphrase and non-paraphrase pairs deliberately chosen to have a high lexical overlap. PAWS-X (Yang et al., 2019) is a multilingual extension of English PAWS. It includes 51401 examples human-translated into German (de), Spanish (es), French (fr), Japanese (ja), Korean (ko) and Chinese (zh).

[1] `https://github.com/adapter-hub/adapter-transformers`

[2] Source: `https://github.com/google-research/bert/blob/master/multilingual.md`

[3] `https://meta.wikimedia.org/wiki/List_of_Wikipedias` (version: 2023/12/15)

XNLI. The Multi-Genre Natural Language Inference (MultiNLI) corpus (Williams et al., 2018) is a multi-genre corpus with the goal of classifying the entailment relation of a pair of sentences. Possible labels are *entailment*, *neutral* or *contradiction*. The corpus contains a total of 432,702 sentence pairs. XNLI (Conneau et al., 2018) extends MultiNLI with human translations into Arabic (ar), Bulgarian (bg), German (de), Greek (el), Spanish (es), French (fr), Hindi (hi), Russian (ru), Swahili (sw), Thai (th), Turkish (tr), Urdu (ur), Vietnamese (vi) and Chinese (zh).

XCOPA. The Choice Of Plausible Alternatives (COPA) dataset (Roemmele et al., 2011; Gordon et al., 2012) is part of the SuperGLUE benchmark (Wang et al., 2019) and consists of 500 training and 500 test examples. Each example consists of a premise, a question (*What was the CAUSE?* or *What happened as a RESULT?*) and two answer options. The task is to select the option that is more likely to have a causal relation with the premise. XCOPA (Ponti et al., 2020) is a multilingual extension that includes human translations of the *evaluation* data into Estonian (et), Haitian Creole (ht), Indonesian (id), Italian (it), Eastern Apurímac Quechua (qu), Kiswahili (sw), Tamil (ta), Thai (th), Turkish (tr), Vietnamese (vi), and Mandarin Chinese (zh).

3.3 Evaluation Setup

For each experiment, we report the mean accuracy over five random seeds. For better comparability across models, we only include the languages from the data sets for which pre-trained language adapters exist on AdapterHub for both models.

4 Results

Given the large number of combinations of models, tasks and language pairs in our experiments, we summarise them and present individual results of particular interest in this section. The full results can be found in Appendix A.

4.1 General Trends

Overall, as we see in table 2 that the $None_{tr}$ model is the best-performing setup. For the individual models, there is however always a similar-performing setup that includes language adapters: For XLM-R, the *Target* setup has the same performance, while for mBERT, the difference to *Source* is negligible (0.1%). For XLM-R, using *Target* has an advantage of 2.4% over *Source*, but for mBERT, it is vice versa with a difference of 2.1%.

	Target	Source	None	$None_{tr}$
XLM-R	**72.6**	70.2	71.0	**72.6**
mBERT	62.7	64.8	59.8	**64.9**

Table 2: Average results for each model over all languages and datasets (XNLI, PAWS-X and XCOPA).

Breaking down the results by datasets, we see in table 3 that the best-performing setup varies notably. All setups except *None* perform best for at least one model-task combination. And while $None_{tr}$ was the best overall, we see that *Target* performs the best on three out of six combinations. Note in this context that the results in table 2 were not adjusted for the number of languages included in the datasets, leading to the smaller PAWS-X set being underrepresented. The difference between *Target* and *None* varies from 0.6% to 5.4%, showing that the reliance of the model on the language adapter is inconsistent.

4.2 Transfer from English

We now zoom into the different target languages, focusing on cross-lingual transfer with English as the source language. This is arguably the most realistic scenario due to the large amount of annotated data available in English. Similar tables for other source languages are presented in Appendix A.

PAWS-X. The results for PAWS-X are reported in table 4. For XLM-R, all setups show a relatively similar performance, with the range of the average across languages being between 77.3% (*English* and *None*) and 78.2% ($None_{tr}$). For mBERT, *None* is an outlier with a strong drop in performance that is consistent across all target languages, getting an accuracy of only 69.4% instead of 76.3-77.4%, while keeping the English source-language adapter is the best setup in all languages.

XNLI. Results for XNLI are reported in table 5. For XLM-R, the $None_{tr}$ setup that is trained and evaluated without language adapters performs best, and this is the case for 7 out of 10 cross-lingual evaluation languages and for English. Comparing *Target* and *Source*, there is a small advantage for using the target-language adapters (on average 70.6 versus 70.0%), but the results are inconsistent over target languages: For 5 evaluation languages, the target-language adapter is better, for 4 languages,

	XLM-R				mBERT			
	Target	Source	None	$None_{tr}$	Target	Source	None	$None_{tr}$
XNLI	72.1	69.4	70.3	**72.4**	60.5	62.9	57.9	**63.3**
PAWS-X	**80.9**	80.1	80.3	80.8	76.7	**78.0**	71.3	77.0
XCOPA	**53.7**	51.9	52.3	50.3	**52.3**	51.3	51.4	51.4

Table 3: Average results for all model-task combinations.

	XLM-R				mBERT			
	Target	English	None	$None_{tr}$	Target	English	None	$None_{tr}$
En	(**91.4**)	(**91.4**)	(91.0)	(91.1)	(**91.3**)	(**91.3**)	(82.7)	(90.4)
De	**83.3**	82.3	82.4	83.2	81.1	**82.2**	73.1	81.2
Es	84.0	**84.1**	83.5	**84.1**	82.0	**83.1**	72.8	81.6
Ja	69.7	69.2	69.6	**70.2**	69.7	**69.9**	64.1	69.1
Zh	74.3	73.7	73.8	**75.1**	72.6	**73.6**	67.8	73.4
Avg.	77.8	77.3	77.3	**78.2**	76.4	**77.2**	69.4	76.3

Table 4: Results on PAWS-X with transfer from English (en) into all evaluated target languages, ordered by pre-training resources top-to-bottom. Results on English are included for reference but excluded from the average.

the English adapter is better, and for one language, they get the same results. For mBERT, keeping the English adapter is the overall best setup with 63.0% (and the best for 9 out of 10 languages), followed by $None_{tr}$ with 62.2%. Exchanging the adapter and especially leaving it out after training can have a strong negative effect for mBERT, showing a higher reliance on the language adapter parameters: The drop when using *None* as compared to using the English adapter that was active during training is 9.4 percentage points.

XCOPA. Results for XCOPA are reported in table 6. For XLM-R, target-language adapters increase the performance consistently compared to all other setups. $None_{tr}$ is the lowest-performing setup by a notable margin (50.3% compared to 52.0-53.8% for the other setups), showing that this model-task combination draws the strongest positive effect from including language adapters in the training. The results for mBERT are more mixed: While *Target* performs best on average, it only performs better than the English adapter for half of the languages. Compared to the other two datasets, exchanging adapters after training does not have a negative impact on mBERT; the English adapter is even the worst on average, while *Target* is the best setup with a margin of 1.0 to 1.1%.

For XLM-R, there are previous results by Pfeiffer et al. (2020b). Our accuracy scores are lower than theirs. However, our results are not directly comparable to theirs as they perform sequential fine-tuning of the task adapter that additionally contains the SIQA dataset, what reportedly improves the performance on XCOPA (Sap et al., 2019).

4.3 Effect of Pre-Training Data

In this section, we contrast the amount of pre-training data of source and target languages by visualising the improvement of using the target-language adapter as compared to keeping the source-language adapter. This is inspired by Pfeiffer et al. (2020b)'s evaluation that finds that adding language adapters helps more for the transfer from high-resource to low-resource languages in named entity recognition. Note that for XCOPA, training data only exists for English, therefore we limit this analysis to PAWS-X and XNLI.

PAWS-X. The cross-lingual transfer for PAWS-X, as seen in Figure 1, does not show a consistent pattern. For mBERT, we see that having a lower-resource source language correlates with a decreased performance with the target-language adapter. It has to be noted though that for this dataset, none of the evaluated languages is particularly low-resource, as we can see in Table 1.

XNLI. For the XNLI data set, we report the results for both models in Figure 2. For XLM-R, we observe a tendency for lower-resource target

	XLM-R				mBERT			
	Target	English	None	None_{tr}	Target	English	None	None_{tr}
En	(81.8)	(81.8)	(81.5)	**(81.7)**	**(78.1)**	**(78.1)**	(70.9)	(77.7)
De	**73.6**	73.3	73.4	**73.6**	66.1	**67.9**	58.1	67.5
Ru	72.4	72.4	72.7	**72.8**	64.1	**64.6**	55.0	64.1
Es	76.0	**76.2**	75.9	75.9	69.1	**71.4**	62.5	70.5
Zh	70.0	**71.7**	70.8	71.0	66.3	**67.4**	57.7	65.8
Vi	71.6	71.5	71.3	**71.8**	68.2	**68.4**	58.7	66.8
Ar	68.6	65.8	68.2	**68.8**	38.7	**62.7**	50.7	61.9
Tr	69.8	70.7	70.2	**71.0**	62.0	**61.3**	50.6	60.4
El	**72.3**	71.9	71.8	72.0	60.8	**60.9**	54.0	60.2
Hi	66.7	67.1	66.9	**67.2**	57.1	**57.4**	47.6	56.5
Sw	65.2	59.0	62.4	**62.7**	37.4	47.7	40.8	**48.2**
Avg.	70.6	70.0	70.4	**70.7**	59.0	**63.0**	53.6	62.2

Table 5: Results on XNLI with transfer from English (en) into all evaluated target languages, ordered by pre-training resources top-to-bottom. Results on English are included for reference but excluded from the average.

	XLM-R				mBERT			
	Target	English	None	None_{tr}	Target	English	None	None_{tr}
Zh	**55.2**	55.0	54.3	49.4	53.7	52.7	**54.2**	53.2
Vi	**55.3**	54.9	55.1	52.8	51.6	52.9	51.1	**52.6**
Tr	**53.1**	51.9	51.2	49.3	51.9	53.2	54.1	**55.6**
Id	**55.7**	53.6	53.4	49.8	50.4	**50.8**	**50.8**	**50.8**
Et	**54.1**	50.7	52.3	51.4	**53.8**	49.3	49.1	51.2
Sw	**54.0**	49.7	52.0	49.7	50.0	50.4	**50.5**	49.1
Ht	**51.2**	48.6	50.6	49.6	**54.6**	52.7	51.2	50.2
Qu	**51.4**	51.2	49.6	50.2	**52.6**	48.5	49.8	48.2
Avg.	**53.8**	52.0	52.3	50.3	**52.3**	51.3	51.4	51.4

Table 6: Results on XCOPA with transfer from English (en) into all evaluated target languages, ordered by pre-training resources top-to-bottom.

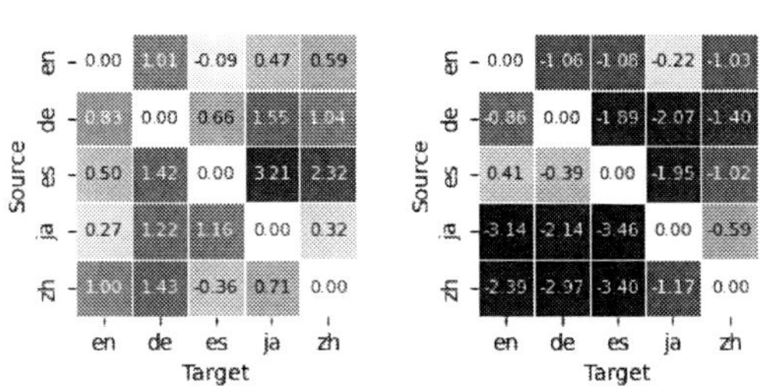

Figure 1: Difference between the target-language adapter and source-language adapter on PAWS-X for XLM-R (left) and mBERT (right) for each source and target language. The amount of pre-training data decreases top-to-bottom/left-to-right.

languages to benefit more, as the right side of the Figure has higher numbers. A strong outlier effect is visible for the lowest-resource language in our evaluation, Swahili, where the gains from the target-language adapter are bigger than for all other target languages by a large margin. Surprisingly, we also see that the benefit of *Target* for English as a source language is smaller than for all other source languages. For mBERT, we do not see a general pattern across all or most of the lower-resource languages. However, with Swahili and Arabic, two outliers show a strongly *negative* effect from their target-language adapters, except when transferred to each other (and, for Swahili, from Russian).

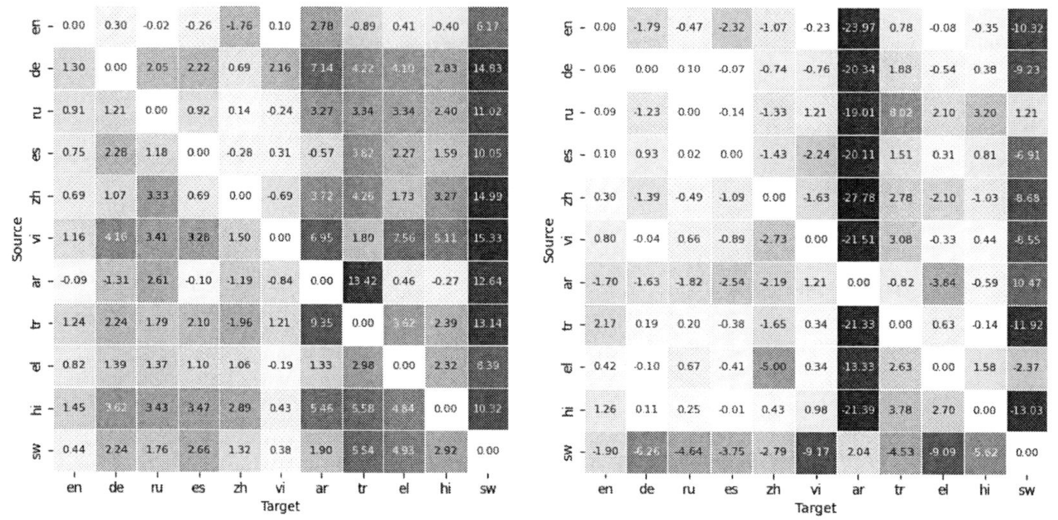

Figure 2: Difference between the target-language adapter and source-language adapter on XNLI with XLM-R (left) and mBERT (right) for each source and target language. The amount of pre-training data decreases top-to-bottom/left-to-right.

5 Discussion

In Section 4 have observed relatively inconsistent results regarding the utility of language adapters, and of target-language adapters in particular. In the following, we discuss the relation of our results to the research questions introduced in Section 1, as well as the variance across datasets, limitations of our experiments, and avenues for future work.

5.1 Effect of Target-Language Adapters (RQ1)

The positive effect of adding a target-language adapter instead of keeping the source-language adapter is inconsistent. While the XLM-R model gains on average 2.4% across all combinations of tasks, source languages and target languages, the mBERT model loses on average 2.1% (Table 2). For the XCOPA dataset, the target-language adapters appear to be crucial to transfer skills, especially for the XLM-R model but to a lesser extent also for mBERT. For the other two datasets, the results are however mixed. Even where the target-language adapter has an advantage, keeping the source-language adapter does not hurt the performance much. This indicates that while zero-shot cross-lingual transfer is possible, for the languages we test on, the performance does not rely much on the target-language adapters. It also indicates that we do not observe a strong isolated modular effect of the language adapters. In line with previous results by He et al. (2021), we hypothesise that much of the target language performance comes from the frozen base model's multilingual capabilities, combined with the task adapter and classification head. This is also confirmed by the finding that no language adapter at all (the *None*$_{tr}$ setup) often performs on par or better than the models with language adapters.

5.2 Reliance on Language Adapters (RQ2)

The drop in performance when removing the language adapter that was included at training time without substitution is weak for XLM-R which loses only 1.6% compared to the *Target* setup and 0.8% compared to the *Source* setup. For mBERT however, it is much stronger, with -2.9% compared to the *Target* and -5.0% compared to the *Source* setup. mBERT appears to be more sensitive to adapter changes after training, indicating that it relies more on the parameters of the language adapters than the relatively robust XLM-R model. However, it does not appear that the language adapter parameters themselves are heavily important, as *None*$_{tr}$ does not see a similar drop. We conclude that the contribution of the language adapters is small.

Related results indicating that the modular role of adapters is inconsistent and not always predictable have been reported by Rücklé et al. (2021) pruning adapters from AdapterFusion models to reduce inference time. They show that this is often possible without sacrificing task performance.

5.3 Effect of Pre-Training Resources (RQ3)

We do not observe a consistent pattern that would indicate that transfer from high-resource to lower-resource languages is more beneficial. In this respect, the NLU benchmarks appear to differ from named entity recognition, where Pfeiffer et al. (2020b) observed a strong effect. That lower-resource languages benefit more is notable for the combination of the XLM-R model and XNLI, but not for the other three model-task combinations. For source languages, we do not see the expected effect; on the contrary, English as the source language has the *worst* record for *Target*. We do however note large differences between language pairs, and outlier languages that benefit or lose more than other languages. This suggests that while language adapters and specifically target-language adapters are not always beneficial, it is worthwhile to test them for every target language individually.

Looking at Quechua, which is not included in the pre-training of either model, and Haitian Creole, which is not included in the pre-training of XLM-R, we observe a positive effect of the target-language adapter. However, both languages are included only in the XCOPA dataset which benefits most from target-language adapters in general, and do not stand out with a higher margin to the *Source* setup than other languages.

5.4 Variance across Datasets

We have observed that for XCOPA, the target-language adapters are more crucial, while for PAWS-X and XNLI, the cross-lingual transfer works similarly well without the language adapter, based on the multilingual capabilities of the pre-trained base model only. A natural question arising from this observation is what causes these differences. One obvious fact is that COPA is a harder task, with models reaching a relatively low performance. In comparison, XNLI is translated from MultiNLI which is reportedly robust to random word-order permutations (Sinha et al., 2021), indicating that lexical cues and less nuanced interactions between words play a large role. This is confirmed by the results of Kew et al. (2023) who compare English versus multilingual instruction fine-tuning of LLMs for cross-lingual transfer and find that for highly structured tasks like XNLI, the language of the fine-tuning plays less of a role. To what extent this is also the case for COPA examples that the models succeed on remains to be tested.

Another hypothesis is that the translations play a role. The translations of XCOPA may be less close to the English source, making a better command of the target language crucial. Closer and more literal translations of PAWS-X and XNLI may enable an easier inheritance of skills learned in English.

5.5 Limitations and Future Work

Architecture. While we do not observe higher increases from *Source* to *Target* for lower-resource languages, there remain large differences in overall performance that correlate with pre-training resources, indicating that cross-lingual transfer is far from a solved problem. The potential of language adapters to narrow this gap has not been exhaustively tested in this work. We have only explored the Pfeiffer adapter architecture and only one single language adapter at a time. As we discussed in Section 2, there are alternative methods which can be explored. The analysis could even be extended with models introducing modularity already at pre-training time (Pfeiffer et al., 2022), which has a different scope but may reveal important insights.

A factor that may limit the potential of language adapters trained post-hoc is the finding that cross-lingual capabilities emerge late in pre-training, as reported by Blevins et al. (2022) doing probing studies on pre-training checkpoints of XLM-R. More work on the interactions of languages in multilingual models, and the prerequisites for successful cross-lingual transfer, may inform the design and training of language adapters in the future.

Languages and Data. Another avenue for future work is a more thorough investigation of adapters for more languages not included in the base model's pre-training. Even adapters for new languages in monolingual models (Artetxe et al., 2020) would be an insightful addition to our analysis. A limiting factor, as in the present work, is the lack of high-quality language understanding benchmarks that cover a broad set of languages. In addition, all datasets we use are translations from the English original, which commonly introduces translation artefacts translation artifacts (Gellerstam, 1986; Freitag et al., 2019). The creation of more such datasets would enable a better understanding of cross-lingual transfer methods.

6 Conclusion

In this work, we performed extensive ablations on cross-lingual transfer with pre-trained language adapters for NLU benchmarks. We found that the inclusion of target-language adapters appears to have a small benefit on average, but it is slight and varies significantly across languages, models and tasks. As the effect is not robust and we do not observe patterns clear enough to predict it, it remains to be tested for each use case and language individually. Keeping the source-language adapter often has a surprisingly good performance, and for one of two models, even leaving out the adapter without substitution is possible without large performance drops. This shows that the model does not rely much on the language adapter, and that language adapters do not appear to be an impactful isolated language module.

While this work provides new insights into the utility of language adapters for NLU, many questions remain open. We conclude that there is a need to identify the specific conditions — such as properties of the base model, task, source, and target languages — under which language adapters enhance performance, and thereby unlocking their usefulness in a broader setting.

Acknowledgments

We thank the anonymous reviewers for their insightful and constructive feedback. The research in this paper was funded by the National Graduate School of Computer Science in Sweden (CUGS) and by the European Commission under grant agreement no. 101135671. The computations were enabled by resources provided by the National Academic Infrastructure for Supercomputing in Sweden (NAISS) at Alvis partially funded by the Swedish Research Council and by the Berzelius resources provided by the Knut and Alice Wallenberg Foundation at the National Supercomputer Centre.

References

Mikel Artetxe, Sebastian Ruder, and Dani Yogatama. 2020. On the cross-lingual transferability of monolingual representations. In *Proceedings of the 58th Annual Meeting of the Association for Computational Linguistics*, pages 4623–4637, Online. Association for Computational Linguistics.

Terra Blevins, Hila Gonen, and Luke Zettlemoyer. 2022. Analyzing the mono- and cross-lingual pretraining dynamics of multilingual language models. In *Proceedings of the 2022 Conference on Empirical Methods in Natural Language Processing*, pages 3575–3590, Abu Dhabi, United Arab Emirates. Association for Computational Linguistics.

Alexis Conneau, Kartikay Khandelwal, Naman Goyal, Vishrav Chaudhary, Guillaume Wenzek, Francisco Guzmán, Edouard Grave, Myle Ott, Luke Zettlemoyer, and Veselin Stoyanov. 2020. Unsupervised cross-lingual representation learning at scale. In *Proceedings of the 58th Annual Meeting of the Association for Computational Linguistics*, pages 8440–8451, Online. Association for Computational Linguistics.

Alexis Conneau and Guillaume Lample. 2019. Cross-lingual language model pretraining. In *Advances in Neural Information Processing Systems*, volume 32. Curran Associates, Inc.

Alexis Conneau, Ruty Rinott, Guillaume Lample, Adina Williams, Samuel Bowman, Holger Schwenk, and Veselin Stoyanov. 2018. XNLI: Evaluating cross-lingual sentence representations. In *Proceedings of the 2018 Conference on Empirical Methods in Natural Language Processing*, pages 2475–2485, Brussels, Belgium. Association for Computational Linguistics.

Jacob Devlin, Ming-Wei Chang, Kenton Lee, and Kristina Toutanova. 2019. BERT: Pre-training of deep bidirectional transformers for language understanding. In *Proceedings of the 2019 Conference of the North American Chapter of the Association for Computational Linguistics: Human Language Technologies, Volume 1 (Long and Short Papers)*, pages 4171–4186, Minneapolis, Minnesota. Association for Computational Linguistics.

Abteen Ebrahimi and Katharina Kann. 2021. How to adapt your pretrained multilingual model to 1600 languages. In *Proceedings of the 59th Annual Meeting of the Association for Computational Linguistics and the 11th International Joint Conference on Natural Language Processing (Volume 1: Long Papers)*, pages 4555–4567, Online. Association for Computational Linguistics.

Fahim Faisal and Antonios Anastasopoulos. 2022. Phylogeny-inspired adaptation of multilingual models to new languages. In *Proceedings of the 2nd Conference of the Asia-Pacific Chapter of the Association for Computational Linguistics and the 12th International Joint Conference on Natural Language Processing (Volume 1: Long Papers)*, pages 434–452, Online only. Association for Computational Linguistics.

Markus Freitag, Isaac Caswell, and Scott Roy. 2019. APE at scale and its implications on MT evaluation biases. In *Proceedings of the Fourth Conference on Machine Translation (Volume 1: Research Papers)*, pages 34–44, Florence, Italy. Association for Computational Linguistics.

Yoshinari Fujinuma, Jordan Boyd-Graber, and Katharina Kann. 2022. Match the script, adapt if multilingual: Analyzing the effect of multilingual pretraining on cross-lingual transferability. In *Proceedings of the 60th Annual Meeting of the Association for Computational Linguistics (Volume 1: Long Papers)*, pages 1500–1512, Dublin, Ireland. Association for Computational Linguistics.

Martin Gellerstam. 1986. Translationese in Swedish novels translated from English. *Translation studies in Scandinavia*, 1:88–95.

Andrew Gordon, Zornitsa Kozareva, and Melissa Roemmele. 2012. SemEval-2012 task 7: Choice of plausible alternatives: An evaluation of commonsense causal reasoning. In **SEM 2012: The First Joint Conference on Lexical and Computational Semantics – Volume 1: Proceedings of the main conference and the shared task, and Volume 2: Proceedings of the Sixth International Workshop on Semantic Evaluation (SemEval 2012)*, pages 394–398, Montréal, Canada. Association for Computational Linguistics.

Ruidan He, Linlin Liu, Hai Ye, Qingyu Tan, Bosheng Ding, Liying Cheng, Jiawei Low, Lidong Bing, and Luo Si. 2021. On the effectiveness of adapter-based tuning for pretrained language model adaptation. In *Proceedings of the 59th Annual Meeting of the Association for Computational Linguistics and the 11th International Joint Conference on Natural Language Processing (Volume 1: Long Papers)*, pages 2208–2222, Online. Association for Computational Linguistics.

Neil Houlsby, Andrei Giurgiu, Stanislaw Jastrzebski, Bruna Morrone, Quentin De Laroussilhe, Andrea Gesmundo, Mona Attariyan, and Sylvain Gelly. 2019. Parameter-efficient transfer learning for NLP. In *Proceedings of the 36th International Conference on Machine Learning*, volume 97 of *Proceedings of Machine Learning Research*, pages 2790–2799. PMLR.

Edward J. Hu, Yelong Shen, Phillip Wallis, Zeyuan Allen-Zhu, Yuanzhi Li, Shean Wang, and Weizhu Chen. 2021. Lora: Low-rank adaptation of large language models. *CoRR*, abs/2106.09685.

Tannon Kew, Florian Schottmann, and Rico Sennrich. 2023. Turning english-centric llms into polyglots: How much multilinguality is needed? *arXiv preprint arXiv:2312.12683*.

Seungwon Kim, Alex Shum, Nathan Susanj, and Jonathan Hilgart. 2021. Revisiting pretraining with adapters. In *Proceedings of the 6th Workshop on Representation Learning for NLP (RepL4NLP-2021)*, pages 90–99, Online. Association for Computational Linguistics.

Anne Lauscher, Vinit Ravishankar, Ivan Vulić, and Goran Glavaš. 2020. From zero to hero: On the limitations of zero-shot language transfer with multilingual Transformers. In *Proceedings of the 2020 Conference on Empirical Methods in Natural Language Processing (EMNLP)*, pages 4483–4499, Online. Association for Computational Linguistics.

Michael McCloskey and Neal J Cohen. 1989. Catastrophic interference in connectionist networks: The sequential learning problem. In *Psychology of learning and motivation*, volume 24, pages 109–165. Elsevier.

Jonas Pfeiffer, Naman Goyal, Xi Lin, Xian Li, James Cross, Sebastian Riedel, and Mikel Artetxe. 2022. Lifting the curse of multilinguality by pre-training modular transformers. In *Proceedings of the 2022 Conference of the North American Chapter of the Association for Computational Linguistics: Human Language Technologies*, pages 3479–3495, Seattle, United States. Association for Computational Linguistics.

Jonas Pfeiffer, Andreas Rücklé, Clifton Poth, Aishwarya Kamath, Ivan Vulić, Sebastian Ruder, Kyunghyun Cho, and Iryna Gurevych. 2020a. AdapterHub: A framework for adapting transformers. In *Proceedings of the 2020 Conference on Empirical Methods in Natural Language Processing: System Demonstrations*, pages 46–54, Online. Association for Computational Linguistics.

Jonas Pfeiffer, Sebastian Ruder, Ivan Vulić, and Edoardo Maria Ponti. 2023. Modular deep learning. *arXiv preprint arXiv:2302.11529*.

Jonas Pfeiffer, Ivan Vulić, Iryna Gurevych, and Sebastian Ruder. 2020b. MAD-X: An Adapter-Based Framework for Multi-Task Cross-Lingual Transfer. In *Proceedings of the 2020 Conference on Empirical Methods in Natural Language Processing (EMNLP)*, pages 7654–7673, Online. Association for Computational Linguistics.

Edoardo Maria Ponti, Goran Glavaš, Olga Majewska, Qianchu Liu, Ivan Vulić, and Anna Korhonen. 2020. XCOPA: A multilingual dataset for causal commonsense reasoning. In *Proceedings of the 2020 Conference on Empirical Methods in Natural Language Processing (EMNLP)*, pages 2362–2376, Online. Association for Computational Linguistics.

Roger Ratcliff. 1990. Connectionist models of recognition memory: constraints imposed by learning and forgetting functions. *Psychological review*, 97(2):285.

Melissa Roemmele, Cosmin Adrian Bejan, and Andrew S Gordon. 2011. Choice of plausible alternatives: An evaluation of commonsense causal reasoning. In *AAAI spring symposium: logical formalizations of commonsense reasoning*, pages 90–95.

Andreas Rücklé, Gregor Geigle, Max Glockner, Tilman Beck, Jonas Pfeiffer, Nils Reimers, and Iryna Gurevych. 2021. AdapterDrop: On the efficiency of adapters in transformers. In *Proceedings of the 2021 Conference on Empirical Methods in Natural Language Processing*, pages 7930–7946, Online and

Punta Cana, Dominican Republic. Association for Computational Linguistics.

Maarten Sap, Hannah Rashkin, Derek Chen, Ronan Le Bras, and Yejin Choi. 2019. Social IQa: Commonsense reasoning about social interactions. In *Proceedings of the 2019 Conference on Empirical Methods in Natural Language Processing and the 9th International Joint Conference on Natural Language Processing (EMNLP-IJCNLP)*, pages 4463–4473, Hong Kong, China. Association for Computational Linguistics.

Koustuv Sinha, Prasanna Parthasarathi, Joelle Pineau, and Adina Williams. 2021. UnNatural Language Inference. In *Proceedings of the 59th Annual Meeting of the Association for Computational Linguistics and the 11th International Joint Conference on Natural Language Processing (Volume 1: Long Papers)*, pages 7329–7346, Online. Association for Computational Linguistics.

Ahmet Üstün, Arianna Bisazza, Gosse Bouma, and Gertjan van Noord. 2020. UDapter: Language adaptation for truly Universal Dependency parsing. In *Proceedings of the 2020 Conference on Empirical Methods in Natural Language Processing (EMNLP)*, pages 2302–2315, Online. Association for Computational Linguistics.

Alex Wang, Yada Pruksachatkun, Nikita Nangia, Amanpreet Singh, Julian Michael, Felix Hill, Omer Levy, and Samuel Bowman. 2019. Superglue: A stickier benchmark for general-purpose language understanding systems. In *Advances in Neural Information Processing Systems*, volume 32. Curran Associates, Inc.

Adina Williams, Nikita Nangia, and Samuel Bowman. 2018. A broad-coverage challenge corpus for sentence understanding through inference. In *Proceedings of the 2018 Conference of the North American Chapter of the Association for Computational Linguistics: Human Language Technologies, Volume 1 (Long Papers)*, pages 1112–1122, New Orleans, Louisiana. Association for Computational Linguistics.

Yinfei Yang, Yuan Zhang, Chris Tar, and Jason Baldridge. 2019. PAWS-X: A cross-lingual adversarial dataset for paraphrase identification. In *Proceedings of the 2019 Conference on Empirical Methods in Natural Language Processing and the 9th International Joint Conference on Natural Language Processing (EMNLP-IJCNLP)*, pages 3687–3692, Hong Kong, China. Association for Computational Linguistics.

Zheng-Xin Yong, Hailey Schoelkopf, Niklas Muennighoff, Alham Fikri Aji, David Ifeoluwa Adelani, Khalid Almubarak, M Saiful Bari, Lintang Sutawika, Jungo Kasai, Ahmed Baruwa, et al. 2022. Bloom+1: Adding language support to bloom for zero-shot prompting. *arXiv preprint arXiv:2212.09535*.

Yuan Zhang, Jason Baldridge, and Luheng He. 2019. PAWS: Paraphrase adversaries from word scrambling. In *Proceedings of the 2019 Conference of the North American Chapter of the Association for Computational Linguistics: Human Language Technologies, Volume 1 (Long and Short Papers)*, pages 1298–1308, Minneapolis, Minnesota. Association for Computational Linguistics.

A Full results

In this section, we present the full results for both models, all three tasks, and all language pairs.

XNLI. For XNLI, we report the results for each source language in the following tables, in decreasing order of the languages' representation in the pre-training corpora of the models: English (Table 7), German (Table 8), Russian (Table 9), Spanish (Table 10), Chinese (Table 11), Vietnamese (Table 12), Arabic (Table 13), Turkish (Table 14), Greek (Table 15), Hindi (Table 16), and Swahili (Table 17). For XLM-R, note the better performance of the Target compared to the Source setup for source languages other than English, which we discussed in section 5.3. For mBERT however, the patterns for the other source languages are similar to the patterns for English.

PAWS-X. For PAWS-X, the results for each source language are found in the following tables, ordered from highest resource to lowest resource: English (Table 18), German (Table 19), Spanish (Table 20), Japanese (Table 21), and Chinese (Table 22). For this dataset, we do not observe major differences between different source languages.

XCOPA. Lastly, for XCOPA, there exists a training set only for English. Therefore, we cannot provide results for other source languages. The results for English are detailed in Table 23.

The impact of source language pre-training resources on the performance. Another observation we would like to draw attention to is the fact that we *do not* observe a tendency that higher-resource source languages lead to a higher performance in cross-lingual transfer: For English as a source language, the best result for XLM-R and XNLI is 70.7% and for mBERT and XNLI, it is 63.0% accuracy. For the lowest-resource language, Swahili, the corresponding numbers are 72.2% accuracy for XLM-R and 61.3% accuracy for mBERT. For PAWS-X, for English, the best result for XLM-R is 78.2%; for mBERT, it is 77.2%. For the lowest-resource language Chinese, the corresponding numbers are higher: 81.9% for XLM-R and 78.6% for mBERT. While the increase is likely to be caused by the fact that the target languages for lower-resource languages are relatively higher-resourced, the patterns we observe show that the amount of pre-training resources of the source language is not of importance for these two datasets.

	XLM-R				mBERT			
	Target	English	None	None_{tr}	Target	English	None	None_{tr}
en	(81.8)	(81.8)	(81.5)	(81.7)	(78.1)	(78.1)	(70.9)	(77.7)
de	73.6	73.3	73.4	73.6	66.1	67.9	58.1	67.5
ru	72.4	72.4	72.7	72.8	64.1	64.6	55.0	64.1
es	76.0	76.2	75.9	75.9	69.1	71.4	62.5	70.5
zh	70.0	71.7	70.8	71.0	66.3	67.4	57.7	65.8
vi	71.6	71.5	71.3	71.8	68.2	68.4	58.7	66.8
ar	68.6	65.8	68.2	68.8	38.7	62.7	50.7	61.9
tr	69.8	70.7	70.2	71.0	62.0	61.3	50.6	60.4
el	72.3	71.9	71.8	72.0	60.8	60.9	54.0	60.2
hi	66.7	67.1	66.9	67.2	57.1	57.4	47.6	56.5
sw	65.2	59.0	62.4	62.7	37.4	47.7	40.8	48.2
Avg.	70.6	70.0	70.4	70.7	59.0	63.0	53.6	62.2

Table 7: Results on XNLI with transfer from English (en) into all evaluated target languages, ordered by pre-training resources top-to-bottom. Results on English are included for reference but excluded from the average.

	XLM-R				mBERT			
	Target	German	None	None_{tr}	Target	German	None	None_{tr}
en	80.0	78.7	79.1	80.5	74.3	74.2	67.9	74.2
de	(76.1)	(76.1)	(74.9)	(75.6)	(71.9)	(71.9)	(65.9)	(71.2)
ru	73.5	71.4	72.7	74.1	66.6	66.5	59.7	66.0
es	76.4	74.1	75.0	76.5	71.5	71.6	64.7	70.9
zh	73.4	72.7	72.9	73.8	67.6	68.4	60.1	67.4
vi	73.5	71.3	72.1	73.4	67.3	68.0	60.2	67.3
ar	70.6	63.4	69.4	71.1	42.0	62.4	53.2	63.7
tr	71.6	67.4	70.9	72.9	62.8	60.9	53.2	61.4
el	73.1	69.0	72.2	73.1	61.6	62.1	55.7	61.8
hi	68.8	65.9	68.5	69.6	58.4	58.0	50.1	58.8
sw	66.7	51.8	63.1	64.2	36.5	45.7	40.3	49.3
Avg.	72.8	68.6	71.6	72.9	60.9	63.8	56.5	64.1

Table 8: Results on XNLI with transfer from German (de) into all evaluated target languages, ordered by pre-training resources top-to-bottom. Results on German are included for reference but excluded from the average.

	XLM-R				mBERT			
	Target	Russian	None	None$_{tr}$	Target	Russian	None	None$_{tr}$
en	80.3	79.4	79.8	80.7	73.3	73.2	69.0	73.5
de	74.5	73.3	73.8	74.9	67.3	68.5	63.3	68.7
ru	(74.7)	(74.7)	(74.0)	(74.9)	(69.5)	(69.5)	(64.2)	(69.4)
es	76.1	75.1	75.8	76.7	70.6	70.8	66.2	70.8
zh	73.3	73.1	72.6	73.3	66.7	68.0	61.0	67.7
vi	73.4	73.7	72.5	73.8	66.9	65.7	62.0	67.7
ar	70.3	67.0	69.6	71.2	38.9	57.9	56.6	63.0
tr	71.5	68.1	71.2	72.2	62.4	54.4	56.3	61.0
el	73.3	70.0	72.9	73.8	60.5	58.4	58.0	61.9
hi	69.4	67.0	68.9	69.6	56.5	53.3	52.1	59.1
sw	67.8	56.7	64.6	64.5	40.2	39.0	44.2	47.2
Avg.	73.0	70.3	72.2	73.1	60.3	60.9	58.9	64.1

Table 9: Results on XNLI with transfer from Russian (ru) into all evaluated target languages, ordered by pre-training resources top-to-bottom. Results on Russian are included for reference but excluded from the average.

	XLM-R				mBERT			
	Target	Spanish	None	None$_{tr}$	Target	Spanish	None	None$_{tr}$
en	80.2	79.5	79.5	80.5	75.4	75.3	71.7	75.0
de	74.0	71.7	73.4	74.8	69.0	68.0	65.2	68.4
ru	72.7	71.5	71.9	73.7	66.5	66.5	61.9	65.3
es	(76.9)	(76.9)	(75.9)	(77.1)	(74.2)	(74.2)	(70.2)	(73.9)
zh	71.4	71.7	71.2	73.0	67.1	68.6	63.0	67.4
vi	72.3	72.0	71.6	73.6	66.1	68.3	63.4	67.5
ar	67.2	67.8	67.7	70.4	42.6	62.7	57.2	62.7
tr	70.6	66.8	70.2	71.9	60.7	59.1	55.3	60.3
el	72.1	69.9	71.4	73.1	62.0	61.7	58.1	61.5
hi	67.7	66.1	67.6	69.1	57.2	56.4	51.9	57.6
sw	65.6	55.5	62.6	63.2	38.1	45.0	45.8	48.3
Avg.	71.4	69.2	70.7	72.3	60.5	63.2	59.4	63.4

Table 10: Results on XNLI with transfer from Spanish (es) into all evaluated target languages, ordered by pre-training resources top-to-bottom. Results on Spanish are included for reference but excluded from the average.

	XLM-R				mBERT			
	Target	Chinese	None	None$_{tr}$	Target	Chinese	None	None$_{tr}$
en	78.7	78.0	77.8	79.0	73.4	73.1	70.9	72.6
de	72.9	71.8	71.4	73.7	66.2	67.6	65.2	67.1
ru	72.3	69.0	70.8	72.6	65.1	65.6	63.4	66.0
es	74.6	73.9	73.5	75.5	69.0	70.1	67.9	69.6
zh	(73.7)	(73.7)	(72.7)	(74.4)	(72.1)	(72.1)	(68.9)	(71.5)
vi	72.5	73.2	71.4	73.5	66.9	68.5	64.8	67.7
ar	68.9	65.2	67.6	69.9	34.7	62.5	59.6	62.3
tr	69.6	65.3	69.4	71.7	61.9	59.2	58.2	60.7
el	71.0	69.2	70.5	72.5	58.3	60.4	58.8	60.5
hi	67.3	64.0	66.8	68.8	57.2	58.3	54.2	58.9
sw	65.6	50.6	62.6	64.0	33.7	42.4	44.9	43.7
Avg.	71.3	68.0	70.2	72.1	58.6	62.8	60.8	62.9

Table 11: Results on XNLI with transfer from Chinese (zh) into all evaluated target languages, ordered by pre-training resources top-to-bottom. Results on Chinese are included for reference but excluded from the average.

	XLM-R				mBERT			
	Target	Vietnamese	None	None$_{tr}$	Target	Vietnamese	None	None$_{tr}$
en	78.3	77.1	76.9	79.5	72.6	71.8	70.0	72.3
de	73.6	69.4	71.0	74.2	66.8	66.8	64.4	66.4
ru	72.6	69.2	69.1	73.5	65.4	64.7	61.9	64.8
es	75.3	72.0	72.4	75.9	69.2	70.1	67.4	69.5
zh	72.5	71.0	70.1	73.3	66.3	69.1	65.9	68.0
vi	(74.7)	(74.7)	(70.9)	(74.8)	(71.0)	(71.0)	(68.5)	(70.3)
ar	69.9	63.0	67.2	70.4	39.5	61.0	58.5	62.0
tr	71.8	70.0	68.4	72.3	63.4	60.3	59.3	60.1
el	72.7	65.1	69.9	73.1	60.8	61.1	60.6	61.9
hi	68.9	63.8	66.8	69.1	58.5	58.1	55.8	57.8
sw	65.7	50.4	61.1	63.5	37.8	46.4	47.1	48.6
Avg.	72.1	67.1	69.3	72.5	60.0	62.9	61.1	63.1

Table 12: Results on XNLI with transfer from Vietnamese (vi) into all evaluated target languages, ordered by pre-training resources top-to-bottom. Results on Vietnamese are included for reference but excluded from the average.

	XLM-R				mBERT			
	Target	Arabic	None	None_{tr}	Target	Arabic	None	None_{tr}
en	78.4	78.4	76.5	79.9	69.6	71.4	63.4	71.4
de	72.5	73.8	69.8	74.5	65.2	66.8	60.0	66.5
ru	71.4	68.8	68.1	73.4	62.5	64.4	57.0	64.0
es	75.0	75.1	72.8	76.3	67.1	69.7	61.8	69.9
zh	71.0	72.1	68.0	72.9	65.1	67.3	60.7	66.5
vi	72.3	73.1	69.0	73.4	64.5	63.3	58.8	66.8
ar	(72.6)	(72.6)	(68.7)	(72.3)	(67.1)	(67.1)	(59.5)	(65.9)
tr	70.2	56.8	66.6	72.1	58.4	59.2	54.3	60.0
el	71.6	71.1	69.8	73.2	58.1	61.9	56.4	61.2
hi	67.4	67.7	65.0	68.8	57.2	57.8	53.0	56.6
sw	66.0	53.4	61.1	63.8	57.5	47.0	44.8	49.0
Avg.	71.6	69.0	68.7	72.8	62.5	62.9	57.0	63.2

Table 13: Results on XNLI with transfer from Arabic (ar) into all evaluated target languages, ordered by pre-training resources top-to-bottom. Results on Arabic are included for reference but excluded from the average.

	XLM-R				mBERT			
	Target	Turkish	None	None_{tr}	Target	Turkish	None	None_{tr}
en	78.1	76.8	75.8	79.0	70.8	68.6	68.3	67.9
de	73.5	71.3	69.6	73.8	66.2	66.0	64.9	65.4
ru	72.4	70.6	67.6	73.4	64.1	63.9	61.8	62.4
es	74.8	72.7	71.2	75.7	66.8	67.2	65.8	66.6
zh	70.2	72.2	65.4	73.3	64.4	66.1	63.1	65.2
vi	72.3	71.1	66.7	73.0	65.8	65.5	62.7	65.1
ar	70.4	61.0	64.5	69.7	39.8	61.1	58.9	61.0
tr	(73.7)	(73.7)	(68.0)	(73.7)	(68.0)	(68.0)	(64.5)	(67.1)
el	71.8	68.1	68.2	72.3	59.9	59.3	59.2	59.9
hi	68.5	66.1	63.8	69.3	58.0	58.1	55.2	57.6
sw	66.2	53.1	58.4	64.8	36.3	48.2	47.2	50.4
Avg.	71.8	68.3	67.1	72.4	59.2	62.4	60.7	62.2

Table 14: Results on XNLI with transfer from Turkish (tr) into all evaluated target languages, ordered by pre-training resources top-to-bottom. Results on Turkish are included for reference but excluded from the average.

	XLM-R				mBERT			
	Target	Greek	None	None_{tr}	Target	Greek	None	None_{tr}
en	79.5	78.7	78.4	79.9	69.3	68.9	64.7	70.6
de	74.6	73.2	73.7	74.7	66.0	66.1	62.1	66.3
ru	73.2	71.9	72.1	73.7	64.2	63.5	60.3	64.8
es	76.5	75.4	75.5	76.5	67.9	68.3	64.3	69.0
zh	72.2	71.1	71.5	73.4	60.0	65.0	60.4	65.3
vi	72.6	72.8	71.3	73.3	64.5	64.2	61.8	65.4
ar	69.9	68.6	69.3	70.9	45.7	59.0	57.3	61.7
tr	70.7	67.8	69.8	71.8	60.5	57.9	55.9	60.5
el	(74.4)	(74.4)	(73.2)	(73.8)	(65.9)	(65.9)	(61.2)	(64.8)
hi	68.3	66.0	67.8	69.2	55.6	54.0	52.2	57.9
sw	67.0	58.6	63.1	64.5	41.0	43.3	45.4	49.2
Avg.	72.5	70.4	71.2	72.8	59.5	61.0	58.4	63.1

Table 15: Results on XNLI with transfer from Greek (el) into all evaluated target languages, ordered by pre-training resources top-to-bottom. Results on Greek are included for reference but excluded from the average.

	XLM-R				mBERT			
	Target	Hindi	None	None_{tr}	Target	Hindi	None	None_{tr}
en	77.7	76.3	76.6	77.3	68.0	66.7	61.7	68.4
de	72.7	69.1	70.4	72.5	64.5	64.4	61.1	64.7
ru	71.7	68.3	69.0	71.8	62.8	62.5	58.8	63.9
es	73.9	70.4	71.8	73.6	66.0	66.0	62.2	65.3
zh	70.7	67.8	68.2	71.2	65.8	65.4	61.7	64.8
vi	71.8	71.4	69.8	71.6	65.9	64.9	61.2	65.3
ar	69.0	63.6	66.3	69.1	36.9	58.2	56.3	60.8
tr	70.9	65.3	68.6	70.9	62.0	58.2	57.4	60.6
el	71.5	66.7	70.1	71.4	60.4	57.7	58.3	60.6
hi	(68.5)	(68.5)	(66.1)	(68.2)	(63.2)	(63.2)	(59.5)	(61.7)
sw	66.3	56.0	61.1	63.1	33.9	46.9	46.5	50.1
Avg.	71.6	67.5	69.2	71.2	58.6	61.1	58.5	62.4

Table 16: Results on XNLI with transfer from Hindi (hi) into all evaluated target languages, ordered by pre-training resources top-to-bottom. Results on Hindi are included for reference but excluded from the average.

	XLM-R				mBERT			
	Target	Swahili	None	None_{tr}	Target	Swahili	None	None_{tr}
en	78.1	77.6	77.2	77.3	67.6	69.5	53.5	67.4
de	73.0	70.7	72.1	72.1	56.6	62.8	47.4	59.6
ru	72.6	70.9	71.1	71.7	58.0	62.7	46.4	61.0
es	74.8	72.1	73.5	73.6	59.7	63.5	49.0	63.2
zh	71.8	70.5	70.7	72.1	60.8	63.6	44.9	61.7
vi	71.8	71.4	70.5	72.4	55.4	64.5	48.7	63.0
ar	68.6	66.7	67.9	69.5	60.7	58.7	42.8	59.0
tr	71.1	65.6	70.1	70.2	50.4	55.0	43.3	55.2
el	71.8	66.9	70.8	70.8	48.7	57.8	44.3	57.1
hi	68.0	65.0	67.3	68.0	49.5	55.1	42.1	52.9
sw	(68.0)	(68.0)	(64.6)	(66.7)	(62.3)	(62.3)	(45.6)	(60.2)
Avg.	72.2	69.7	71.1	71.8	56.7	61.3	46.2	60.0

Table 17: Results on XNLI with transfer from Swahili (sw) into all evaluated target languages, ordered by pre-training resources top-to-bottom. Results on Swahili are included for reference but excluded from the average.

	XLM-R				mBERT			
	Target	English	None	None_{tr}	Target	English	None	None_{tr}
en	(91.4)	(91.4)	(91.0)	(91.1)	(91.3)	(91.3)	(82.7)	(90.4)
de	83.3	82.3	82.4	83.2	81.1	82.2	73.1	81.2
es	84.0	84.1	83.5	84.1	82.0	83.1	72.8	81.6
ja	69.7	69.2	69.6	70.2	69.7	69.9	64.1	69.1
zh	74.3	73.7	73.8	75.1	72.6	73.6	67.8	73.4
Avg.	77.8	77.3	77.3	78.2	76.4	77.2	69.4	76.3

Table 18: Results on PAWS-X with transfer from English (en) into all evaluated target languages, ordered by pre-training resources top-to-bottom. Results on English are included for reference but excluded from the average.

	XLM-R				mBERT			
	Target	German	None	None_{tr}	Target	German	None	None_{tr}
en	90.1	89.3	89.4	89.8	86.9	87.8	80.7	86.2
de	(84.5)	(84.5)	(83.9)	(84.3)	(81.6)	(81.6)	(74.3)	(81.0)
es	84.3	83.6	83.7	84.2	78.9	80.8	74.3	79.8
ja	71.0	69.4	70.6	71.6	66.4	68.4	64.0	68.9
zh	75.2	74.2	75.0	75.1	71.7	73.1	68.8	72.0
Avg.	80.1	79.1	79.7	80.2	76.0	77.5	72.0	76.7

Table 19: Results on PAWS-X with transfer from German (de) into all evaluated target languages, ordered by pre-training resources top-to-bottom. Results on German are included for reference but excluded from the average.

	XLM-R				mBERT			
	Target	Spanish	None	None_{tr}	Target	Spanish	None	None_{tr}
en	90.1	89.6	89.6	89.9	88.1	87.7	77.9	87.2
de	83.5	82.1	82.4	82.9	80.3	80.7	68.5	80.5
es	(86.4)	(86.4)	(84.4)	(85.0)	(83.0)	(83.0)	(67.6)	(83.1)
ja	70.9	67.7	69.4	70.4	67.3	69.2	62.2	69.5
zh	75.4	73.0	74.6	75.0	71.8	72.8	63.9	72.6
Avg.	80.0	78.1	79.0	79.6	76.9	77.6	68.1	77.4

Table 20: Results on PAWS-X with transfer from Spanish (es) into all evaluated target languages, ordered by pre-training resources top-to-bottom. Results on Spanish are included for reference but excluded from the average.

	XLM-R				mBERT			
	Target	Japanese	None	None_{tr}	Target	Japanese	None	None_{tr}
en	87.3	87.0	86.9	87.2	74.9	78.0	73.1	75.4
de	82.0	80.8	81.4	81.7	72.3	74.4	70.7	71.7
es	81.4	80.2	80.9	82.7	72.2	75.7	71.7	73.2
ja	(74.3)	(74.3)	(73.5)	(73.7)	(72.1)	(72.1)	(68.8)	(71.5)
zh	77.3	77.0	77.4	77.1	73.5	74.1	69.7	72.6
Avg.	82.0	81.2	81.6	82.2	73.2	75.6	71.3	73.2

Table 21: Results on PAWS-X with transfer from Japanese (ja) into all evaluated target languages, ordered by pre-training resources top-to-bottom. Results on Japanese are included for reference but excluded from the average.

	XLM-R				mBERT			
	Target	Chinese	None	None_{tr}	Target	Chinese	None	None_{tr}
en	88.7	87.7	88.3	88.7	80.7	83.1	77.2	81.7
de	82.6	81.1	81.9	82.2	76.0	79.0	72.7	76.9
es	82.3	82.7	82.5	83.6	76.5	79.9	74.7	78.2
ja	73.2	72.4	72.8	73.1	71.2	72.4	67.6	71.4
zh	(78.4)	(78.4)	(78.0)	(78.0)	(76.1)	(76.1)	(72.4)	(75.6)
Avg.	81.7	81.0	81.4	81.9	76.1	78.6	73.1	77.1

Table 22: Results on PAWS-X with transfer from Chinese (zh) into all evaluated target languages, ordered by pre-training resources top-to-bottom. Results on Chinese are included for reference but excluded from the average.

	XLM-R				mBERT			
	Target	English	None	None_{tr}	Target	English	None	None_{tr}
zh	55.2	55.0	54.3	49.4	53.7	52.7	54.2	53.2
vi	55.3	54.9	55.1	52.8	51.6	52.9	51.1	52.6
tr	53.1	51.9	51.2	49.3	51.9	53.2	54.1	55.6
id	55.7	53.6	53.4	49.8	50.4	50.8	50.8	50.8
et	54.1	50.7	52.3	51.4	53.8	49.3	49.1	51.2
sw	54.0	49.7	52.0	49.7	50.0	50.4	50.5	49.1
ht	51.2	48.6	50.6	49.6	54.6	52.7	51.2	50.2
qu	51.4	51.2	49.6	50.2	52.6	48.5	49.8	48.2
Avg.	53.8	52.0	52.3	50.3	52.3	51.3	51.4	51.4

Table 23: Results on XCOPA with transfer from English (en) into all evaluated target languages, ordered by pre-training resources top-to-bottom.

Mixing and Matching: Combining Independently Trained Translation Model Components

Taido Purason and **Andre Tättar** and **Mark Fishel**
University of Tartu, Estonia
{taido,andre,mark}@tartunlp.ai

Abstract

This paper investigates how to combine encoders and decoders of different independently trained NMT models. Combining encoders/decoders is not directly possible since the intermediate representations of any two independent NMT models are different and cannot be combined without modification. To address this, firstly, a dimension adapter is added if the encoder and decoder have different embedding dimensionalities, and secondly, representation adapter layers are added to align the encoder's representations for the decoder to process. As a proof of concept, this paper looks at many-to-Estonian translation and combines a massively multilingual encoder (NLLB) and a high-quality language-specific decoder. The paper successfully demonstrates that the sentence representations of two independent NMT models can be made compatible without changing the pre-trained components while keeping translation quality from deteriorating. Results show significant improvements in both translation quality and speed for many-to-one translation over the baseline multilingual model.

1 Introduction

As the availability of pre-trained models continuously increases, there is a growing need to investigate how to use them efficiently. Previous works have looked at effectively using pre-trained neural machine translation (NMT) models by effective fine-tuning (Bapna and Firat, 2019; Zhu et al., 2021) as well as using pre-trained language models in NMT model training (Zhu et al., 2020; Rothe et al., 2020; Chen et al., 2021; Sun et al., 2021; Chen et al., 2022).

This paper examines the feasibility of combining together components (like encoders and decoders) of independent pre-trained NMT models without any retraining or fine-tuning. We investigate how representations of independently trained models can be made compatible and evaluate the resulting translation quality and efficiency. Surprisingly, our evaluation shows that the resulting combined model can surpass the original models in translation quality and speed.

Combining any pre-trained encoder and decoder poses two problems. Firstly, their representation spaces will not be compatible, as the models are trained independently. Secondly, the embedding dimension of the representation can also differ across any two pre-trained models. We propose a method that solves both issues and allows the encoder and decoder of any pre-trained NMT models to be combined. Specifically, in our architecture (Figure 1), we use a small adapter to convert the dimensionality and representation space of the encoder to something the decoder is trained to process. In order for the adapter to learn its weights, the whole pipeline (Encoder A - adapter - Decoder B) is trained in an end-to-end fashion, except both the encoder and decoder are frozen. Thus, the only part changing the weights is the adapter itself while the original components remain intact.

As a proof of concept, we investigate combining encoders and decoders of multiple different pre-trained NMT models, focusing on an output language-specific scenario. In other words, a highly multilingual encoder is combined with a monolingual decoder, tuned to high performance on a single

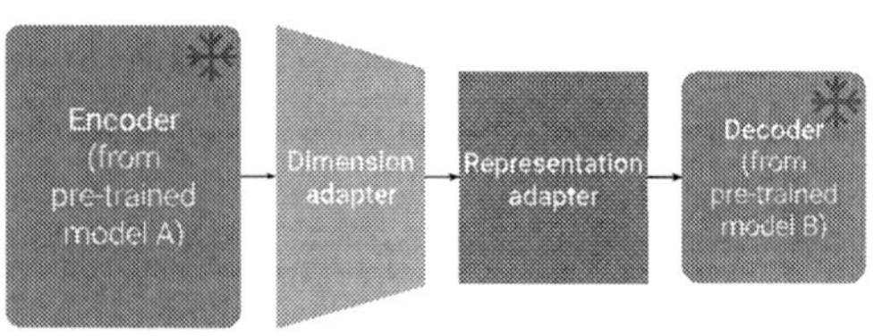

Figure 1: The proposed mix-and-match architecture. Dimension adapter is a component that takes input with the dimensionality of model A output and outputs with the dimensionality of model B (for example a linear transformation). Adapter layers are transformer encoder layers. Components from models A and B have frozen parameters.

Proceedings of the 1st Workshop on Modular and Open Multilingual NLP (MOOMIN 2024), pages 44–56
March 21, 2024 ©2024 Association for Computational Linguistics

language. Since highly multilingual models often suffer from the capacity bottleneck (Johnson et al., 2017; Tan et al., 2019; Arivazhagan et al., 2019), we hypothesize that adding a high-quality language-specific decoder can improve the translation quality to the language of the decoder. Furthermore, translation to one language requires less capacity than many-to-many scenarios and thus would potentially require fewer parameters, resulting in faster translation.

Using NLLB (Team et al., 2022) as the multilingual model and MTee (Tättar et al., 2022) as the language-specific Estonian model, we demonstrate significant improvements in translation quality over the baseline NMT model for many-to-Estonian translation and show competitive results to pivoting and fine-tuning. Our method is not only effective to train compared to traditional fine-tuning but also provides a reduction in running costs of the translation model thanks to the number of parameters being reduced by 40% compared to the baseline NLLB model.

The main contributions of this work are:

- a novel method for combining pre-trained NMT models, which improves translation quality, is effective to train, and reduces the model's parameters (Section 3);
- a detailed ablation of the proposed method, exploring the effect of freezing or unfreezing different involved components, comparing simpler and more complicated adapter architectures, and involving more source languages in training (Section 4);
- an open-source implementation of our proposed method (see subsection 3.5).

2 Related Work

To the best of our knowledge, creating new NMT models by connecting encoders and decoders of different pre-trained NMT models has not been explored yet. Similar approaches have been tested in speech translation (Li et al., 2021; Gállego et al., 2021). Similarity between independently learned representations has been explored between linguistic, image representations as well as brain waves (Søgaard, 2023; Li et al., 2023), however we attempt direct conversion and exploitation of these representations.

2.1 Pre-trained NMT models

There are many pre-trained NMT models already openly available for use. OpusMT provides over 1000 NMT models, most of which are bilingual, but some also multilingual (Tiedemann and Thottingal, 2020). Rothe et al. (2020) published NMT models which were initialized from BERT and trained on the NMT task. M2M-100 is a series of NMT models (varying in size) which were trained on 7.5B sentence pairs and support translation between 100 languages (Fan et al., 2020). The NLLB-200 NMT model further improves it and extends support to 200 languages with a training dataset of 18B sentence pairs (Team et al., 2022). Both M2M-100 and NLLB-200 are strong baselines in NMT research regarding translation quality. MTee provides an Estonian-centric (Estonian to/from English, German, Russian) NMT model with language-specific encoders-decoders (Tättar et al., 2022). The most recent contribution to massively multilingual models is MADLAD-400 (Kudugunta et al., 2023), with both decoder-only as well as sequence-to-sequence models with both the encoder and decoder released. Finally, large multilingual language models like GPT-3 and GPT-4 have demonstrated an ability to translate (Brown et al., 2020; Bubeck et al., 2023), however they only demonstrate highly competitive quality for high-resource languages.

2.2 Multilingual NMT

Recently, there have been numerous advancements in multilingual NMT. One of the most widely followed approaches is demonstrated by Johnson et al. (2017), where they use a single (universal) model with shared vocabulary for multilingual NMT, which enables transfer learning and zero-shot translation. Massively multilingual training has since been successfully demonstrated (Aharoni et al., 2019; Arivazhagan et al., 2019; Zhang et al., 2020). Additionally, fine-tuning methods of NMT models have been investigated, including lightweight fine-tuning methods such as adapters (Bapna and Firat, 2019; Zhu et al., 2021). In addition to universal models, there has been successful research into modular multilingual NMT using language-specific encoders and decoders (Escolano et al., 2021; Lyu et al., 2020). As an alternative to supporting all directions in the models, pivoting (translating through a pivot language) has also been used as a method for achieving higher quality multilingual translation (Habash and Hu, 2009).

2.3 Pre-trained Language Models for NMT

With many pre-trained language models (LMs) becoming available, making use of them in NMT has become an important topic.

The first line of works takes the approach of pre-training an encoder-decoder model for seq2seq tasks and then fine-tuning the model for MT, for example, mBART (Liu et al., 2020), and MASS (Song et al., 2019).

In the second approach, the encoder or the decoder can be trained independently and later used in an NMT model. Zhu et al. (2020) incorporates input sentence representations into an NMT model. Rothe et al. (2020) initializes NMT model's encoder and/or decoder weights from pre-trained language models. SixT (Chen et al., 2021) used XLM-R as the pre-trained encoder in combination with a randomly initialized decoder, trained using 2-stage training where first the decoder is trained (rest of the model frozen) and secondly, the rest of the model is tuned. This was further improved and expanded in SixT+ (Chen et al., 2022). Sun et al. (2021) combined a BERT-like encoder and a GPT-like decoder into a single model by adding extra layers to both the encoder and decoder.

Ma et al. (2021) uses aspects of both approaches by initializing an encoder-decoder model from an encoder-only language model and pre-training on seq2seq tasks before fine-tuning for MT.

Li et al. (2021) combines a pre-trained audio encoder and pre-trained decoder from mBART to create a speech translation model through fine-tuning.

3 Approach and Setup

3.1 Methodology

Our approach combines two pre-trained NMT models using an adapter placed "between" the encoder and decoder: see Figure 1). The adapter consists of a dimension adapter and representation adapter.

The dimension adapter is a linear transformation (feed-forward layer) with input dimensionality equal to the encoder embedding dimension and the output dimensionality to the decoder embedding dimension. We place the dimension adapter directly after the pre-trained encoder.

Representation adapter layers are implemented as randomly initialized transformer layers. They have the same embedding dimension as the decoder. We do not modify the decoder by adding extra layers or other parameters; thus it is kept lightweight, leading to fast translation using beam search since encoder embeddings are calculated once for a sentence, but the decoder is used repeatedly.

Training: when training the model, the adapter learns with the rest of the components in an end-to-end fashion. Training examples are passed through the whole pipeline (encoder, then adapter, then decoder), however both the encoder and decoder remain frozen. Thus the only weights that are allowed to change are the parts of the adapter.

We also perform reverse-ablation and compare our original approach of freezing all but the adapter to less efficient alternatives of also letting the decoder tune itself during training, randomly initializing the decoder as well as tuning the whole model. A combination of the originally proposed approach (tuning only the adapter) and then continuing training the adapter and an unfrozed pre-initialized decoder will be referred to as the 2-stage approach.

3.2 Translation models

We rely on *NLLB-1B-distilled* as the pre-trained model for encoders in our experiments (referred to in the further text as NLLB-1B or NLLB); Section 4.3.3 also includes a comparison to *NLLB-600M-distilled* as the base model. For the decoder, we use the Estonian decoder from MTee (Tättar et al., 2022) – a modular model with language-specific encoders and decoders (encoders/decoders follow transformer base architecture (Vaswani et al., 2017)).

The pre-trained NLLB-1B encoder has 24 layers with an embedding dimension of 1024 and a feed-forward dimension of 8192. In the main experiments, we add a linear dimension adapter that transforms the embedding dimension from 1024 to 512 and 4 representation adapter layers with the same embedding and feed-forward dimension as the decoder (512 and 2048 respectively) to the encoder.

3.3 Dataset

We use English-Estonian (22M, sentence pairs), German-Estonian (12.5M sentence pairs), French-Estonian (11.7M sentence pairs), and Polish-Estonian (7M sentence pairs) directions from CC-Matrix (Schwenk et al., 2019). In Ablation Section 4.3.3 we use Europarl (Tiedemann, 2012).

We use SentencePiece (SP) (Kudo and Richardson, 2018) models from the respective pre-trained NMT models for segmenting the data. For example when we use NLLB encoder and MTee decoder, we use NLLB SP model for processing the source and MTee SP model for processing the target.

The models are evaluated using FLORES-200 (Team et al., 2022) *devtest* as the test set and *dev* as the validation set. The same directions the model is trained on are used for validation. The best checkpoint, according to the validation loss, is used for test set evaluation. Test set evaluation is carried out on all 201 many-to-Estonian directions. We confirmed that the test set was not present in the training data of MTee and also trust that since FLORES-200 was the main test set of NLLB (Team et al., 2022), it would be properly cleaned from their training dataset.

3.4 Evaluation

For evaluation we mainly rely on chrF++[1] (Popović, 2017), but also report chrF[2] (Popović, 2015) for comparison with previous research. We use the sacreBLEU (Post, 2018) implementation.

Although BLEU (Papineni et al., 2002) is a widely adopted metric, several evaluation campaigns (Barrault et al., 2021; Koehn et al., 2022) have shown its weaker correlation with human judgements of translation quality compared to chrF/chrF++ and neural metrics like COMET (Rei et al., 2020). However, we still include BLEU scores for comparison in Appendix A. Additionally, we provide COMET scores (Rei et al., 2020) for a selection of languages in Appendix B.

For the main experiments, we conduct 5 random restarts for each model and report the mean score with a confidence interval ($p = 0.01$, t-distribution). We also report the Win Rate with Significance (WRS) – the percentage of language pairs where the model outperforms the baseline (NLLB-1B) with significance $p = 0.01$. The significance is tested using a one-sample one-tailed t-test for experiments with 5 seeds. Additionally, we report WRS based on a single seed with significance calculated with paired bootstrap resampling (PBR) (Koehn, 2004).

3.5 Implementation and training

We use Fairseq (Ott et al., 2019) for implementing training. Additionally, we made our specific implementation of training and models public[3].

For the main experiments, all models are trained for a total of 100k updates. If 2-stage training is used, the first stage is trained for 50k updates and the second stage for 50k updates. The learning rate used is 0.0005 for the first stage and 0.0001 for the second stage. We use Adam optimizer (Kingma and Ba, 2015). An inverse square root learning rate scheduler with 4000 warm-up steps is used for all experiments. We use dropout and attention dropout of 0.1. Models are trained with mixed precision (*fp16*). All translations are acquired using beam search with beam size 4.

The models were trained on 8 GPUs for the main experiments. The batch size was 4096 tokens per GPU. The training was performed on the LUMI supercomputer[4], utilizing 4 AMD Instinct MI250X 128GB HBM2e (each acting as 2 GPUs).

4 Results

4.1 Main Results

The main results are reported in Table 1. *NLLB-1B-distilled* is used as a baseline. Additionally, results of the largest publicly available NLLB model (NLLB-MoE) with 54.5B parameters reported by Team et al. (2022) are used for comparison. The table lists average chrF++ scores over all many-to-Estonian translation directions and all official EU languages[5]. The EU language averages are reported to highlight the translation quality for languages more closely related to Estonian and also more frequently translated from. We analyze the quantitative results of pivoting, fine-tuning, and our mixing and matching approach of combining the encoder and the decoder of different pre-trained models.

4.1.1 Pivoting

NLLB-1B English pivoting for many-to-Estonian translation results in an average 1.2 chrF++ point improvement across all directions, significantly outperforming the baseline NLLB-1B model on 84.6% of directions (see (3) in Table 1). When NLLB-1B is used to translate to English and MTee is used for English-to-Estonian translation (see (4) in Table 1), the translation quality is improved by 3.2 chrF++

[1]sacreBLEU signature: `nrefs:1|case:mixed|eff:yes|nc:6|nw:2|space:no|version:2.3.1`

[2]sacreBLEU signature: `nrefs:1|case:mixed|eff:yes|nc:6|nw:0|space:no|version:2.3.1`

[3]https://anonymous.4open.science/r/mix-and-match-nmt

[4]https://www.lumi-supercomputer.eu/

[5]Bulgarian, Croatian, Czech, Danish, Dutch, English, Estonian, Finnish, French, German, Greek, Hungarian, Irish, Italian, Latvian, Lithuanian, Maltese, Polish, Portuguese, Romanian, Slovak, Slovenian, Spanish, and Swedish

	Model	Parameters			Train.	average chrF++ ↑		WRS (%) ↑	
		train	total	eff.	time	full	EU	t-test	PBR
(1)	NLLB-1B	-	1.37B	1.37B	-	40.2	46.7	-	-
(2)	NLLB-MoE†	-	54.5B	54.5B	-	43.0	49.6	-	99.5
	Pivot, m2en: NLLB-1B								
(3)	en2et NLLB-1B	-	1.37B	2.74B	-	41.4	47.5	-	84.6
(4)	en2et: MTee	-	1.42B	1.42B	-	**43.4**	50.2	-	**100.0**
	Fine-tune NLLB-1B								
(5)	-	1.37B	1.37B	1.37B	22.3	42.5 ± 0.1	50.1 ± 0.3	91.0	86.6
(6)	freeze enc	604M	1.37B	1.37B	15.0	43.0 ± 0.1	50.3 ± 0.2	**98.0**	98.5
	Ours: NLLB-1B enc +								
(7)	rand dec	51M	817M	817M	4.4	42.6 ± 0.3	50.2 ± 0.3	93.5	97.5
(8)	MTee dec	13M	817M	817M	3.9	42.5 ± 0.1	50.4 ± 0.1	92.0	89.1
(9)	MTee dec, 2-stage	51M	817M	817M	4.1	43.1 ± 0.1	**50.9 ± 0.1**	93.0	96.5

Table 1: Many-to-Estonian translation average chrF++ scores. Additionally model training, total and effective parameters and training time (hours) is reported. Effective parameter count represents the number of parameters used during translation. For experiments involving model training, the average of 5 random seeds is reported with confidence intervals ($p = 0.01$). Average chrF++ is reported for all directions and official EU languages separately. WRS (Win Rate with significance, $p = 0.01$) reports what percentage of directions outperform the baseline with both significance based on t-test on 5 seeds and significance based on paired bootstrap resampling t-test (PBR). † - Scores reported by (Team et al., 2022).

points on average compared to the baseline (1), significantly outperforming it on all directions. These results demonstrate that pivoting can enhance translation quality without additional training. However, pivoting requires passing through two models, which increases the time required for translation and reduces long-term cost efficiency.

4.1.2 Fine-tuning

We experimented with two different fine-tuning strategies: full fine-tuning (5) and fine-tuning only the decoder of the baseline NLLB model with the encoder frozen (6). We found that both approaches lead to significant improvements over the baseline: 2.3 and 2.8 chrF++ points, respectively. Moreover, fine-tuning exhibited superior performance compared to the baseline across more language pairs, as confirmed by the t-test WRS scores: 98.0% for the frozen encoder method vs. 91.0% for full fine-tuning.

4.1.3 Mixing and Matching

When NLLB encoder and MTee decoder are combined with adapter layers, by only training the adapter (13M parameters) and freezing the pre-trained components, the resulting model (NLLB enc + MTee dec model (8)) significantly outperforms the baseline on 92.0% of the directions according to the t-test (89.1% according to PBR), with an average improvement of 2.3 chrF++ points. The 2-stage training approach (9) – training the adapter first (13M parameters), followed by training the adapter with the decoder (51M parameters) – achieved the best results. This method (9) outperforms the baseline by 2.9 chrF++ points on average across all directions and achieves similar average chrF++ scores to the 54B parameter NLLB model. It is only slightly behind the best-performing pivoting model in terms of average chrF++ scores. Additionally, we observed that the 2-stage training approach significantly outperforms the baseline on 93% of the language pairs according to the t-test (96.5% according to the PBR). However, the fine-tuning method with a frozen encoder showed significant improvements over the baseline in 5% more directions than our approach.

We also evaluated a decoder that was randomly initialized with the same architecture and vocabulary as MTee (7), and trained in a single stage with a frozen encoder, only training the adapter and decoder. It outperformed the baseline by 2.4 chrF++ points on average. This method performs similarly to the initialized model with no decoder training. Although it is still slightly outperformed by the 2-stage model with the pre-initialized decoder in terms of the average chrF++ score, it can be useful when a high-quality pre-trained decoder model is unavailable.

Average BLEU scores are presented in Appendix A Table 6, since they support the same conclusions as the chrF++ scores.

Model	eng_Latn	deu_Latn	rus_Cyrl	zho_Hans	arb_Arab
NLLB-1B	52.6	48.5	46.6	40.2	45.8
NLLB-MoE†	56.1	51.8	49.5	43.8	49.1
MTee	56.9	52.2	49.9	-	-
Pivot, m2en: NLLB-1B					
en2et NLLB-1B	52.6	48.7	47.2	42.4	46.8
en2et: MTee	56.9	52.4	49.8	**45.5**	**49.5**
Fine-tune NLLB-1B					
-	56.6 ± 0.3	52.3 ± 0.5	50.1 ± 0.2	44.5 ± 0.2	48.8 ± 0.2
freeze enc	56.2 ± 0.4	52.3 ± 0.3	50.1 ± 0.2	44.6 ± 0.2	48.8 ± 0.2
Ours: NLLB-1B enc +					
rand dec	56.1 ± 0.4	52.0 ± 0.5	49.8 ± 0.5	44.1 ± 0.3	48.6 ± 0.3
MTee dec	56.7 ± 0.5	52.4 ± 0.4	49.9 ± 0.3	43.5 ± 0.3	48.6 ± 0.2
MTee dec 2-stage	**57.3 ± 0.3**	**52.8 ± 0.2**	**50.4 ± 0.3**	44.6 ± 0.4	49.1 ± 0.3

Table 2: Many-to-Estonian translation chrF++ scores for selected directions. Confidence intervals are based on 5 random seeds. † - Scores reported by Team et al. (2022). Language abbreviations following Team et al. (2022).

For EU languages, NLLB-enc+MTee-dec, 2-stage (9) achieves the highest average chrF++ score and outperforms the baseline by 4.2 chrF++ points. This shows that our method achieves the best result for more closely related languages, whereas the pivoting approach of combining two models was better for more distant languages. A possible explanation could be the training data being composed of EU languages. Furthermore, the pre-trained decoder was also trained with two EU languages and Russian as input, which could contribute to the high performance on translating EU languages.

In Table 2, we present the chrF++ scores for translations from a selection of languages to Estonian, serving as an example. It also shows the comparison with the MTee model for the languages supported by the pre-trained MTee model. The mix-and-match models (ours) perform similarly to the MTee model, with the 2-stage model outperforming MTee slightly. It can also be seen that for Chinese and Arabic, our approach is outperformed by pivoting with NLLB and MTee. This further suggests that our method produces better translation quality for closer related languages. We also provide COMET scores for these directions in Appendix B, which support mostly the same conclusions, except for NLLB-MoE scores, which rank the highest among the models.

4.1.4 Efficiency

The mix-and-match method (NLLB-1B enc. + MTee dec.) reduces the number of parameters by 40% compared to the baseline model and the default fine-tuning approach. Even though we add 13M trainable parameters to the encoder (adapter layers), we use a significantly smaller decoder than NLLB-1B, leading to fewer trained and total parameters. This makes the training time of our method (4.1 hours for NLLB-enc+MTee-dec, 2-stage) 5.4 times faster than the full fine-tuning (22.3 hours). Furthermore, the inference with NLLB-enc+MTee-dec is approximately 6.5 times faster than with NLLB-1B. This demonstrates that our approach offers an efficient and cost-effective alternative to fine-tuning and pivoting that delivers comparable or better translation quality, with the added benefit of faster training (compared to fine-tuning), fewer parameters, and faster inference.

4.2 Ukrainian-Estonian Translation

Model	chrF ↑
NLLB-1B	50.9
NLLB-MoE†	54.0
NLLB-MTee EN pivot	54.5
NLLB-enc+MTee-dec	54.6 ± 0.2
NLLB-enc+MTee-dec, 2-stage	**55.0 ± 0.1**
Bergmanis and Pinnis (2022)	53.5

Table 3: Ukrainian (Cyrillic) to Estonian (Latin) translation chrF scores on FLORES-101 *devtest*. NLLB-1B model was used for all experiments, except for NLLB-MoE (54B). † - calculated from translations reported by (Team et al., 2022).

We demonstrate that without needing Ukrainian-Estonian data, we can rapidly create a model with competitive translation quality. We compare scores of our best model with work by Bergmanis and Pinnis (2022) and report chrF to be compatible with their evaluation. We can see that our best model

(NLLB-enc+MTee-dec, 2-stage) outperforms their Ukrainian to Estonian model by 1.5 chrF points (see Table 3). It also outperforms the NLLB-1B baseline by 4.1 chrF points and achieves a slightly higher score than NLLB-MoE and pivoting with NLLB-1B and MTee.

4.3 Ablation

4.3.1 Effect of multi-stage training

We look at additional training strategies in addition to training adapter or adapter and decoder. It can be seen in Table 4 that training only the adapter and decoder yields the best results both in single-stage and multi-stage training strategies. Strategies involving encoder training take longer to train due to more trained parameters and do not yield any visible benefit. We can hypothesize that it is because the encoder is already trained for the domain of the test set. We can see that the 2-stage training, which trains the adapter in the first stage and the adapter and decoder in the second stage, produces the best scoring model and is also the second fastest behind the single-stage model, which trains only the adapter. While encoder training did not yield improvements for the current pre-trained models, training and test datasets, it might yield different results if these elements differ. For example, when pre-trained models are trained for a domain different from the training and test datasets, fine-tuning the encoder might be necessary.

Training setup dec. init.	stage		Trained params	Time (hrs)	chrF++ avg
	single				
random	A+D		51M	4.3	42.8
MTee	A+D		51M	4.4	42.9
MTee	A		13M	3.8	42.4
	I	II			
random	A+D	E+A+D	817M	5.5	42.7
MTee	A	A+D	51M	4.0	43.2
MTee	A	E+A	779M	7.5	42.1
MTee	A	E+A+D	817M	7.2	42.8

Table 4: Comparison of training strategies. chrF++ scores as calculated on FLORES200 *devtest*. All models listed have 817M total parameters. Trained parameters are based on the last stage and models follow the NLLB-1B+MTee mix-and-match model structure. The stage column describes which parameters are trained. A - dim. adapter and adapter layers, D - decoder, E - encoder. The results are based on a single seed.

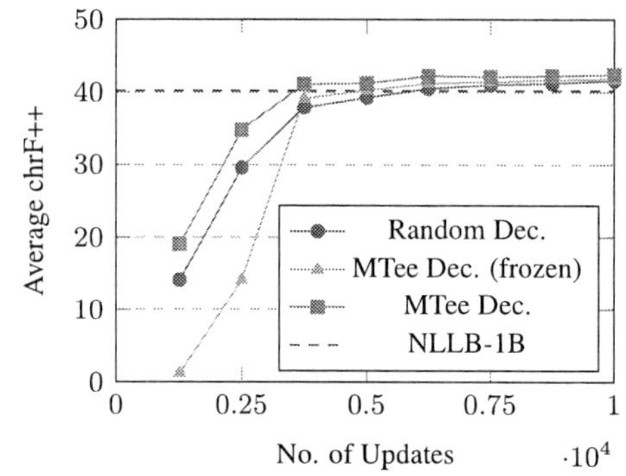

Figure 2: Average test chrF++ score for NLLB+MTee models for first 10,000 training updates (evaluated every 1250 updates). Decoder and adapter (dimensional and layers) are trained, with the rest of the encoder frozen, unless specified with frozen.

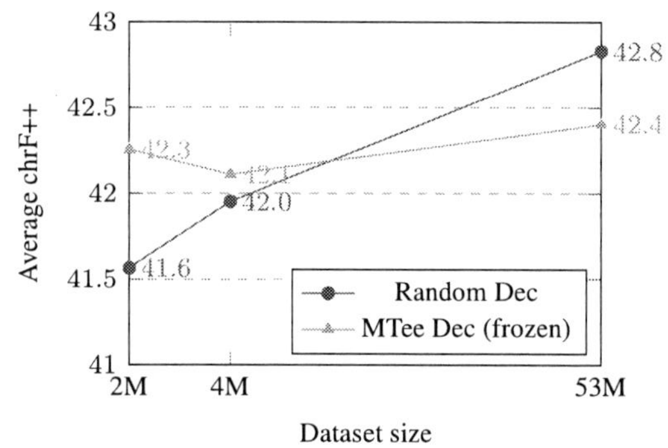

Figure 3: Average test chrF++ score for NLLB+MTee models for three dataset sizes: 500k sentence pairs per direction (2M in total), 1M per direction (4M in total) and the whole dataset (53M in total) trained for 100k updates. For MTee Dec model only dimensional adapter and adapter layers are trained, while the decoder and encoder remain frozen.

4.3.2 Effect of the pre-trained decoder

Since we saw that using a pre-trained decoder had a result close to using a randomly initialized decoder, we investigated further how fast the models converge and how the results would compare using less training data.

From Figure 2, we can see that surprisingly for the first 2500 updates the model with a pre-trained encoder and decoder, which trains only the adapter converges the slowest, even being behind the randomly initialized decoder. However, when the decoder is not frozen, we can see that it converges faster than with an uninitialized decoder.

For the dataset size, we can see on Figure 3 that the model with pre-trained encoder and decoder models is less affected by the dataset size, compared to the model that only uses a pre-trained encoder.

4.3.3 Effect of adapter structure and the number of languages

	Model			chrF++↑
	NLLB-600M baseline			36.6
	NLLB-600M + MTee			
	adapter config	DA type	src langs	
(1)	DA	MLP	2	35.7 ± 0.2
(2)	DA	linear	2	34.6 ± 0.3
(3)	DA + AL	MLP	2	35.7 ± 2.3
(4)	DA + AL	linear	2	38.2 ± 0.3
(5)	DA + 2 AL	MLP	2	38.0 ± 1.9
(6)	DA + 2 AL	linear	2	38.7 ± 0.3
(7)	2 AL + DA	linear	2	38.3 ± 0.9
(8)	AL + DA + AL	linear	2	38.5 ± 0.2
(9)	DA + 2 AL	linear	4	38.9 ± 0.1
(10)	DA + 2 AL	linear	6	38.9 ± 0.1
(11)	DA + 3 AL	linear	4	39.0 ± 0.1
(12)	DA + 4 AL	linear	4	39.1 ± 0.1
(13)	DA + 5 AL	linear	4	39.0 ± 0.2

Table 5: Many-to-Estonian translation average chrF++ scores of ablation models trained on Europarl evaluated on FLORES200 *devtest*. DA - dimension adapter, AL - adapter layer, DA + n AL means dimension adapter followed by n adapter layers. Training set source languages used are EN, DE, FR, PL, LV, FI, added in the same order when number of languages is increased.

Experiments in this section are performed on the Europarl dataset with results reported in Table 5. The models are trained for 20 epochs on 1 GPU.

It can be seen that using only a dimension adapter without any added layers does not yield as good results and adding layers significantly increases the chrF++ score (see experiments 1–6 in Table 5). Additionally, we see that using the MLP dimension adapter instead of linear yields better results when only using the dimension adapter, but when adding layers it is less stable, resulting in higher variance in average chrF++ scores and lower scores in general.

We can also see that changing the position of the dimension adapter in relation to the adapter layers (to the middle or to the end) does not result in any benefit (see experiments 7 – 9 vs 6).

Using 4 languages results in slightly higher scores than 2 languages (experiments 8 vs 9), however, there is no significant difference when using 6 languages compared to 4 (experiments 9 vs 10). The increase in chrF++ scores could also be caused by the larger dataset and not require different languages to be achieved.

Using 4 layers yields the best result, although the difference in chrF++ scores is small and might not be significant when compared to other numbers of layers (see experiments 11 – 13).

5 Conclusion

We have demonstrated that different pre-trained models can be successfully combined even if they have different architectures that wouldn't be directly compatible. With our method, the pre-trained models can remain unchanged while the added dimension adapter and adapter layers align the embeddings. However, in our experiments, the best results were obtained by continuing decoder training after initial adapter training. This might differ in other scenarios depending on the dataset, pre-trained models, and desired translation domain. Our method allowed for a 40% reduction in parameters, efficient training, fast translation, and increased translation quality compared to the original models. With this in mind, we can think of pre-trained translation model encoders and decoders as modules that can be combined depending on the desired outcome.

6 Future Works

Our focus is on many-to-one translation. However, it should also be investigated how the mix-and-match approach could be used in one-to-many or many-to-many (or many-to-few) scenarios. The proposed method should also be investigated for other more specific domains and other languages apart from Estonian. Additionally, it should be investigated how other parameter-efficient methods compare to this approach and how they could be incorporated into this method. Further comparisons with pre-trained language models and a combination of using LM and NMT models need exploring as well. Finally, this approach of making sequence representations compatible is not limited to NMT and could be applied to other tasks and modalities.

7 Acknowledgements

This work was partially supported by the Estonian Research Council grant PRG2006 as well as the National Programme of Estonian Language Technology grant EKTB67. All computations were performed on the LUMI Supercomputer through the University of Tartu's HPC center.

8 Limitations

One potential limiting factor of the proposed approach is the evaluation process. To ensure accurate and fair evaluation of the models, it is necessary to possess knowledge of the data on which the model was trained to avoid issues with leaky test data. The evaluation of our results relied primarily on automatic metrics, and we mainly utilized the FLORES-200 *devtest* due to the limited availability of test sets for Estonian and non-English languages. Additionally, we were unable to confirm that other available test sets were not part of the original models' training data, so we could not use them for a fair evaluation.

Moreover, the applicability of the mix-and-match method is dependent on the availability of pre-trained models in the target language. For instance, while Estonian models were readily available, other languages may not have such models, rendering the proposed method inapplicable. However, as an alternative, we proposed training the decoder from scratch and demonstrated its competitive performance.

It should also be noted that the translation quality results for Estonian cannot be generalized to all other languages. For example, English already exhibits high translation quality in most multilingual pre-trained NMT models, hence our method may not significantly improve performance as it would for Estonian. However, this limitation does not detract from other positive aspects of our method, including reduced parameter count and efficient training.

Ethics Statement

From an environmental standpoint, our method reduces the training time, giving a significant one-time reduction. Since our scenario also created a smaller model with faster translation, it reduces long-term computation costs.

From the social standpoint, the resulting models might still be suffering from the same kind of biases as the original models and this aspect is yet to be evaluated. However, with our methods, we can make the use of pre-trained models accessible to more people in terms of computational costs.

References

Roee Aharoni, Melvin Johnson, and Orhan Firat. 2019. Massively multilingual neural machine translation. In *Proceedings of the 2019 Conference of the North American Chapter of the Association for Computational Linguistics: Human Language Technologies, Volume 1 (Long and Short Papers)*, pages 3874–3884, Minneapolis, Minnesota. Association for Computational Linguistics.

Naveen Arivazhagan, Ankur Bapna, Orhan Firat, Dmitry Lepikhin, Melvin Johnson, Maxim Krikun, Mia Xu Chen, Yuan Cao, George Foster, Colin Cherry, Wolfgang Macherey, Zhifeng Chen, and Yonghui Wu. 2019. Massively multilingual neural machine translation in the wild: Findings and challenges.

Ankur Bapna and Orhan Firat. 2019. Simple, scalable adaptation for neural machine translation. In *Proceedings of the 2019 Conference on Empirical Methods in Natural Language Processing and the 9th International Joint Conference on Natural Language Processing (EMNLP-IJCNLP)*, pages 1538–1548, Hong Kong, China. Association for Computational Linguistics.

Loic Barrault, Ondrej Bojar, Fethi Bougares, Rajen Chatterjee, Marta R. Costa-jussa, Christian Federmann, Mark Fishel, Alexander Fraser, Markus Freitag, Yvette Graham, Roman Grundkiewicz, Paco Guzman, Barry Haddow, Matthias Huck, Antonio Jimeno Yepes, Philipp Koehn, Tom Kocmi, Andre Martins, Makoto Morishita, and Christof Monz, editors. 2021. *Proceedings of the Sixth Conference on Machine Translation*. Association for Computational Linguistics, Online.

Toms Bergmanis and Marcis Pinnis. 2022. From zero to production: Baltic-ukrainian machine translation systems to aid refugees. *Baltic Journal of Modern Computing*, 10(3):271–282.

Tom Brown, Benjamin Mann, Nick Ryder, Melanie Subbiah, Jared D Kaplan, Prafulla Dhariwal, Arvind Neelakantan, Pranav Shyam, Girish Sastry, Amanda Askell, Sandhini Agarwal, Ariel Herbert-Voss, Gretchen Krueger, Tom Henighan, Rewon Child, Aditya Ramesh, Daniel Ziegler, Jeffrey Wu, Clemens Winter, Chris Hesse, Mark Chen, Eric Sigler, Mateusz Litwin, Scott Gray, Benjamin Chess, Jack Clark, Christopher Berner, Sam McCandlish, Alec Radford, Ilya Sutskever, and Dario Amodei. 2020. Language models are few-shot learners. In *Advances in Neural Information Processing Systems*, volume 33, pages 1877–1901. Curran Associates, Inc.

Sébastien Bubeck, Varun Chandrasekaran, Ronen Eldan, Johannes Gehrke, Eric Horvitz, Ece Kamar, Peter Lee, Yin Tat Lee, Yuanzhi Li, Scott Lundberg, Harsha Nori, Hamid Palangi, Marco Tulio Ribeiro, and Yi Zhang. 2023. Sparks of artificial general intelligence: Early experiments with gpt-4.

Guanhua Chen, Shuming Ma, Yun Chen, Li Dong, Dongdong Zhang, Jia Pan, Wenping Wang, and Furu Wei. 2021. Zero-shot cross-lingual transfer of neural machine translation with multilingual pretrained encoders. In *Proceedings of the 2021 Conference on Empirical Methods in Natural Language Processing*, pages 15–26, Online and Punta Cana, Dominican Republic. Association for Computational Linguistics.

Guanhua Chen, Shuming Ma, Yun Chen, Dongdong Zhang, Jia Pan, Wenping Wang, and Furu Wei. 2022. Towards making the most of cross-lingual transfer for zero-shot neural machine translation. In *Proceedings of the 60th Annual Meeting of the Association for Computational Linguistics (Volume 1: Long Papers)*, pages 142–157, Dublin, Ireland. Association for Computational Linguistics.

Carlos Escolano, Marta R. Costa-jussà, José A. R. Fonollosa, and Mikel Artetxe. 2021. Multilingual machine translation: Closing the gap between shared and language-specific encoder-decoders. In *Proceedings of the 16th Conference of the European Chapter of the Association for Computational Linguistics: Main Volume*, pages 944–948, Online. Association for Computational Linguistics.

Angela Fan, Shruti Bhosale, Holger Schwenk, Zhiyi Ma, Ahmed El-Kishky, Siddharth Goyal, Mandeep Baines, Onur Celebi, Guillaume Wenzek, Vishrav Chaudhary, Naman Goyal, Tom Birch, Vitaliy Liptchinsky, Sergey Edunov, Edouard Grave, Michael Auli, and Armand Joulin. 2020. Beyond English-Centric Multilingual Machine Translation.

Gerard I. Gállego, Ioannis Tsiamas, Carlos Escolano, José A. R. Fonollosa, and Marta R. Costa-jussà. 2021. End-to-end speech translation with pre-trained models and adapters: UPC at IWSLT 2021. In *Proceedings of the 18th International Conference on Spoken Language Translation (IWSLT 2021)*, pages 110–119, Bangkok, Thailand (online). Association for Computational Linguistics.

Nizar Habash and Jun Hu. 2009. Improving Arabic-Chinese statistical machine translation using English as pivot language. In *Proceedings of the Fourth Workshop on Statistical Machine Translation*, pages 173–181, Athens, Greece. Association for Computational Linguistics.

Melvin Johnson, Mike Schuster, Quoc V. Le, Maxim Krikun, Yonghui Wu, Zhifeng Chen, Nikhil Thorat, Fernanda Viégas, Martin Wattenberg, Greg Corrado, Macduff Hughes, and Jeffrey Dean. 2017. Google's multilingual neural machine translation system: Enabling zero-shot translation. *Transactions of the Association for Computational Linguistics*, 5:339–351.

Diederik P. Kingma and Jimmy Lei Ba. 2015. Adam: A method for stochastic optimization.

Philipp Koehn. 2004. Statistical significance tests for machine translation evaluation. In *Proceedings of the 2004 Conference on Empirical Methods in Natural Language Processing*, pages 388–395, Barcelona, Spain. Association for Computational Linguistics.

Philipp Koehn, Loïc Barrault, Ondřej Bojar, Fethi Bougares, Rajen Chatterjee, Marta R. Costa-jussà, Christian Federmann, Mark Fishel, Alexander Fraser, Markus Freitag, Yvette Graham, Roman Grundkiewicz, Paco Guzman, Barry Haddow, Matthias Huck, Antonio Jimeno Yepes, Tom Kocmi, André Martins, Makoto Morishita, Christof Monz, Masaaki Nagata, Toshiaki Nakazawa, Matteo Negri, Aurélie Névéol, Mariana Neves, Martin Popel, Marco Turchi, and Marcos Zampieri, editors. 2022. *Proceedings of the Seventh Conference on Machine Translation (WMT)*. Association for Computational Linguistics, Abu Dhabi, United Arab Emirates (Hybrid).

Taku Kudo and John Richardson. 2018. SentencePiece: A simple and language independent subword tokenizer and detokenizer for neural text processing. In *Proceedings of the 2018 Conference on Empirical Methods in Natural Language Processing: System Demonstrations*, pages 66–71, Brussels, Belgium. Association for Computational Linguistics.

Sneha Kudugunta, Isaac Caswell, Biao Zhang, Xavier Garcia, Christopher A. Choquette-Choo, Katherine Lee, Derrick Xin, Aditya Kusupati, Romi Stella, Ankur Bapna, and Orhan Firat. 2023. Madlad-400: A multilingual and document-level large audited dataset.

Jiaang Li, Yova Kementchedjhieva, and Anders Søgaard. 2023. Implications of the convergence of language and vision model geometries.

Xian Li, Changhan Wang, Yun Tang, Chau Tran, Yuqing Tang, Juan Pino, Alexei Baevski, Alexis Conneau, and Michael Auli. 2021. Multilingual speech translation from efficient finetuning of pretrained models. In *Proceedings of the 59th Annual Meeting of the Association for Computational Linguistics and the 11th International Joint Conference on Natural Language Processing (Volume 1: Long Papers)*, pages 827–838, Online. Association for Computational Linguistics.

Yinhan Liu, Jiatao Gu, Naman Goyal, Xian Li, Sergey Edunov, Marjan Ghazvininejad, Mike Lewis, and Luke Zettlemoyer. 2020. Multilingual denoising pretraining for neural machine translation. *Transactions of the Association for Computational Linguistics*, 8:726–742.

Sungwon Lyu, Bokyung Son, Kichang Yang, and Jaekyoung Bae. 2020. Revisiting Modularized Multilingual NMT to Meet Industrial Demands. In *Proceedings of the 2020 Conference on Empirical Methods in Natural Language Processing (EMNLP)*, pages 5905–5918, Online. Association for Computational Linguistics.

Shuming Ma, Li Dong, Shaohan Huang, Dongdong Zhang, Alexandre Muzio, Saksham Singhal, Hany Hassan Awadalla, Xia Song, and Furu Wei. 2021. DeltaLM: Encoder-Decoder Pre-training for

Language Generation and Translation by Augmenting Pretrained Multilingual Encoders.

Myle Ott, Sergey Edunov, Alexei Baevski, Angela Fan, Sam Gross, Nathan Ng, David Grangier, and Michael Auli. 2019. fairseq: A fast, extensible toolkit for sequence modeling. In *Proceedings of the 2019 Conference of the North American Chapter of the Association for Computational Linguistics (Demonstrations)*, pages 48–53, Minneapolis, Minnesota. Association for Computational Linguistics.

Kishore Papineni, Salim Roukos, Todd Ward, and Wei-Jing Zhu. 2002. Bleu: a method for automatic evaluation of machine translation. In *Proceedings of the 40th Annual Meeting of the Association for Computational Linguistics*, pages 311–318, Philadelphia, Pennsylvania, USA. Association for Computational Linguistics.

Maja Popović. 2015. chrF: character n-gram F-score for automatic MT evaluation. In *Proceedings of the Tenth Workshop on Statistical Machine Translation*, pages 392–395, Lisbon, Portugal. Association for Computational Linguistics.

Maja Popović. 2017. chrF++: words helping character n-grams. In *Proceedings of the Second Conference on Machine Translation*, pages 612–618, Copenhagen, Denmark. Association for Computational Linguistics.

Matt Post. 2018. A call for clarity in reporting BLEU scores. In *Proceedings of the Third Conference on Machine Translation: Research Papers*, pages 186–191, Brussels, Belgium. Association for Computational Linguistics.

Ricardo Rei, Craig Stewart, Ana C Farinha, and Alon Lavie. 2020. COMET: A neural framework for MT evaluation. In *Proceedings of the 2020 Conference on Empirical Methods in Natural Language Processing (EMNLP)*, pages 2685–2702, Online. Association for Computational Linguistics.

Sascha Rothe, Shashi Narayan, and Aliaksei Severyn. 2020. Leveraging pre-trained checkpoints for sequence generation tasks. *Transactions of the Association for Computational Linguistics*, 8:264–280.

Holger Schwenk, Guillaume Wenzek, Sergey Edunov, Edouard Grave, and Armand Joulin. 2019. Ccmatrix: Mining billions of high-quality parallel sentences on the web. *arXiv preprint arXiv:1911.04944*.

Kaitao Song, Xu Tan, Tao Qin, Jianfeng Lu, and Tie-Yan Liu. 2019. Mass: Masked sequence to sequence pre-training for language generation. In *International Conference on Machine Learning*, pages 5926–5936.

Zewei Sun, Mingxuan Wang, and Lei Li. 2021. Multilingual translation via grafting pre-trained language models. In *Findings of the Association for Computational Linguistics: EMNLP 2021*, pages 2735–2747, Punta Cana, Dominican Republic. Association for Computational Linguistics.

Anders Søgaard. 2023. Grounding the vector space of an octopus: Word meaning from raw text. *Minds & Machines*, 33:33—54.

Xu Tan, Yi Ren, Di He, Tao Qin, and Tie-Yan Liu. 2019. Multilingual neural machine translation with knowledge distillation. In *International Conference on Learning Representations*.

NLLB Team, Marta R. Costa-jussà, James Cross, Onur Çelebi, Maha Elbayad, Kenneth Heafield, Kevin Heffernan, Elahe Kalbassi, Janice Lam, Daniel Licht, Jean Maillard, Anna Sun, Skyler Wang, Guillaume Wenzek, Al Youngblood, Bapi Akula, Loic Barrault, Gabriel Mejia Gonzalez, Prangthip Hansanti, John Hoffman, Semarley Jarrett, Kaushik Ram Sadagopan, Dirk Rowe, Shannon Spruit, Chau Tran, Pierre Andrews, Necip Fazil Ayan, Shruti Bhosale, Sergey Edunov, Angela Fan, Cynthia Gao, Vedanuj Goswami, Francisco Guzmán, Philipp Koehn, Alexandre Mourachko, Christophe Ropers, Safiyyah Saleem, Holger Schwenk, and Jeff Wang. 2022. No language left behind: Scaling human-centered machine translation.

Jörg Tiedemann and Santhosh Thottingal. 2020. OPUS-MT — Building open translation services for the World. In *Proceedings of the 22nd Annual Conferenec of the European Association for Machine Translation (EAMT)*, Lisbon, Portugal.

Jörg Tiedemann. 2012. Parallel data, tools and interfaces in opus. In *Proceedings of the Eight International Conference on Language Resources and Evaluation (LREC'12)*, Istanbul, Turkey. European Language Resources Association (ELRA).

Andre Tättar, Taido Purason, Hele-Andra Kuulmets, Agnes Luhtaru, Liisa Rätsep, Maali Tars, Mārcis Pinnis, Toms Bergmanis, and Mark Fishel. 2022. Open and competitive multilingual neural machine translation in production. in: Proceedings of baltic hlt 2022. *Baltic Journal of Modern Computing*, 10(3):422434.

Ashish Vaswani, Noam Shazeer, Niki Parmar, Jakob Uszkoreit, Llion Jones, Aidan N Gomez, Ł ukasz Kaiser, and Illia Polosukhin. 2017. Attention is all you need. In *Advances in Neural Information Processing Systems*, volume 30. Curran Associates, Inc.

Biao Zhang, Philip Williams, Ivan Titov, and Rico Sennrich. 2020. Improving massively multilingual neural machine translation and zero-shot translation. In *Proceedings of the 58th Annual Meeting of the Association for Computational Linguistics*, pages 1628–1639, Online. Association for Computational Linguistics.

Jinhua Zhu, Yingce Xia, Lijun Wu, Di He, Tao Qin, Wengang Zhou, Houqiang Li, and Tieyan Liu. 2020. Incorporating bert into neural machine translation. In *International Conference on Learning Representations*.

Yaoming Zhu, Jiangtao Feng, Chengqi Zhao, Mingxuan Wang, and Lei Li. 2021. Counter-interference adapter for multilingual machine translation. In *Findings of the Association for Computational Linguistics: EMNLP 2021*, pages 2812–2823, Punta Cana, Dominican Republic. Association for Computational Linguistics.

A BLEU Scores

Average BLEU scores are presented in Table 6

B COMET Scores for Selected Directions

COMET scores of selected directions are displayed in Table 7.

	Model	average BLEU ↑	
		full	EU
(1)	NLLB-1B	12.8	16.9
(2)	NLLB-MoE†	15.5	20.1
	Pivot, m2en: NLLB-1B		
(3)	en2et NLLB-1B	13.5	17.3
(4)	en2et: MTee	**15.7**	20.4
	Fine-tune NLLB-1B		
(5)	-	15.4 ± 0.1	20.8 ± 0.2
(6)	freeze enc	15.5 ± 0.1	20.8 ± 0.1
	Ours: NLLB-1B enc +		
(7)	rand dec	14.5 ± 0.1	19.8 ± 0.1
(8)	MTee dec	15.1 ± 0.1	20.6 ± 0.2
(9)	MTee dec, 2-stage	15.6 ± 0.1	**21.3 ± 0.1**

Table 6: Many-to-Estonian translation average BLEU scores. For experiments involving model training, the average of 5 random seeds are reported with confidence intervals ($p = 0.01$). † - Scores reported by (Team et al., 2022).

Model	eng_Latn	deu_Latn	rus_Cyrl	zho_Hans	arb_Arab
NLLB-1B	0.8967	0.8805	0.8700	0.8435	0.8492
NLLB-MoE†	**0.9144**	**0.9031**	**0.8904**	**0.8826**	**0.8781**
MTee	0.8916	0.8908	0.8819	-	-
Pivot, m2en NLLB-1B					
en2et NLLB-1B	0.8967	0.8808	0.8705	0.8673	0.8583
en2et MTee	0.8916	0.8899	0.8782	0.8788	0.8615
Fine-tune NLLB-1B					
-	0.8954	0.8878	0.8825	0.8775	0.8631
freeze enc	0.8974	0.8912	0.8812	0.8772	0.8552
Ours: NLLB-1B enc +					
rand dec	0.9001	0.8902	0.8793	0.8688	0.8561
MTee dec	0.9049	0.8953	0.8831	0.8659	0.8586
MTee dec 2-stage	0.9060	0.8929	0.8857	0.8724	0.8607

Table 7: Many-to-Estonian translation COMET scores for selected directions. Underlined results indicate a significant gain over the baseline NLLB-1B with $p = 0.01$ according to Paired Bootstrap Resampling t-test. † - Scores calculated from translations reported by Team et al. (2022). Language abbreviations are following Team et al. (2022).

Author Index

Association for Computational Linguistics
209 N. Eighth Street
Stroudsburg, Pennsylvania 18360

ISBN 978-1-7138-9456-8

CURRAN ASSOCIATES INC.
proceedings.com